EX
LIBRIS

*Esther Brewer*

# EXTRA
# SPIRITUAL
# POWER

# EXTRA SPIRITUAL POWER

## ▓ SECOND SIGHT
## AND THE CHRISTIAN

## ▓ DON GILMORE

WORDBOOKS, PUBLISHER, WACO, TEXAS

All Scripture quotations, unless otherwise noted, are from the Revised Standard Version of the Bible, copyright 1946 and 1952 by the Division of Christian Education of the National Council of the Churches of Christ in the United States of America, and are used by permission.

Quotations marked Phillips are from J. B. Phillips, *The New Testament in Modern English,* copyright 1958, 1959, 1960, by J. B. Phillips, published by The Macmillan Company.

The quotation marked TEV is from *Good News for Modern Man,* Today's English Version of the New Testament, copyright © American Bible Society 1966.

The quotation from Loren Eiseley, *The Immense Journey,* copyright © 1946, 1950, 1951, 1953, 1956, 1957 by Loren Eiseley, is used by permission of the publisher, Random House.

The quotation from Christopher Fry, *A Sleep of Prisoners,* copyright ©1951 by Christopher Fry, is used by permission of the publisher, Oxford University Press.

First Printing—May, 1972
Second Printing—July, 1972

FOR
*Johnny Ell*
*Howard* and *Bettie Ell*
whose lives inspired this book

# CONTENTS

# ■1

## SECOND SIGHT
## AND THE NEW AGE

"I feel I am ripe. The time of spiritual exploration is now. My accustomed paths of worn-out patterns are no longer tolerable. Something is in the wind—like the discovery of something so bright it will be out of the spectrum range. I can't give this up because everything is riding on it—all my hopes, aspirations, dreams, goals, philosophy, theology—everything! Everything! I must find my head. I must find my eyes. I want to see! I want to know!"

—My brother John, aged 28.

# SECOND SIGHT
# AND THE NEW AGE

It was the first day of spring. Pressured for time, I was hurrying across a college campus, wondering why I had ever agreed to address a student conference thirty minutes after arriving at the local airport that was, as I recall, twenty-five unfamiliar miles away. My host had assured me, "Just rent a car, follow my directions, and you'll have no problems."

Ordinarily I'm not a pessimist about such things, but this time I knew I was going to be late. Nothing was going right. A berserk, gusty wind seemed intent on blowing dust in my eyes, messing my hair, and pushing against all my anxious effort to get where I was going on time. The noontime sun, unfettered in a cloudless sky, was unseasonably hot. I remember being hot and sticky in a heavy, blue flannel suit, and to make matters worse I was rapidly losing confidence in my hastily transcribed directions. Something inside kept insisting that I was headed the wrong way, but at this late date there was nothing to do but hurry and hope.

Suddenly, a girl with long dark hair stood blocking my way on the narrow path, holding a cluster of yellow daffodils. I have no idea where she came from . . . perhaps she knew me from somewhere. Anyhow as I attempted to push by, she said the most ridiculous thing—"If you'll smile, I'll give you a flower."

I stopped and stared at her, emotionally suspended between indignation and embarrassment. At that late moment the last thing I needed was to be the object of someone's sick sense of humor. Ignoring the flower thrust in my direction, I gave her a dark look and started on my way. Unfortunately, I made the mistake of looking back and caught a glimpse of my image reflected in the wide mirror of her strangely discerning eyes. There I was, a visiting campus preacher, stern-faced, doggedly plowing forward come hell or high water—to get before an audience and speak on the subject "Christ-love Is the Answer." There she was, offering a symbol of good will, wearing a Christlike expression. I was *trying* to be. She was *being*. It was an odious comparison.

In an attempt to make amends for my brusqueness, I accepted her daffodil, explained why I was visiting her school, and asked that she point me toward the place I was supposed to be. She seemed intrigued that I was a minister (people often are), and agreed not only to tell me how to reach my destination but, even better, volunteered to escort me there. We fell into step easily and eventually I asked a typical clergy-type question, mostly because a significant lull had developed in our conversation.

"Do you belong to some religious group on campus?"

I can still see her face, more accurately her eyes, now unforgettable because I have seen them many times since in diverse places. At the risk of sounding unduly romantic, the eyes nearly always seem to be filled with a marvelous sense of openness and curiosity that captivates some and alarms others.

"I'm a new age Christian," she answered.

"A new what?" One gets accustomed to hearing the familiar sounds—Baptist, Catholic, Congregationalist, Episcopalian, Methodist, Presbyterian, United Church, etc. But not . . .

"I'm a new age Christian."

"Do you mean 'new age' like the age of Aquarius?"

Apparently I had drawn the wrong conclusion. A strained silence drifted between us that seemed to last longer than it actually did. Then with a swift flow of words she clarified her position.

"I don't like being put in any one bag including Aquarius, because I'm more than that. Like some of my friends are called 'Jesus freaks' just because they believe in Jesus. I'm against stereotypes of any kind because they limit the ways people can approach each other. If you lump me with all the other people you think of as Aquarians, then you'll have a closed mind concerning whatever else I am."

She spoke with such authority and persuasiveness that for the moment I had forgotten my race against the clock. We were no longer half running—our pace had slowed considerably.

"All right," I agreed. "You are unique. But when most people hear the words 'new age,' they are as nervous as a college chaplain friend of mine who said: 'This sort of thing [a discussion of the new age] is like watching the funnel cloud of a tornado off in the distance and wondering which way it will go next.' The new age image in the minds of many people is a whole witches' brew of negative things —like freaking out on drugs, campus unrest, murder at a rock festival, breakdown of moral values, disregard for tradition, bizarre dress, political revolution, and in general raising hell with the Establishment."

There was another lengthy pause as my new age companion seemed to be checking off what I had said by an inner point of reference. I remained silent not wishing to disturb her thought.

"In my opinion, what you've just said is very negative." Her voice was a bit brittle. "I can't deny the existence of the things you've just mentioned, but what about all the positive things that are happening? Do you realize that a genuine spiritual revolution is going on in this country, and those who ought to be most aware of it are least tuned in because it's not going on in very many churches?" I felt the burn of her words. "Maybe this is because new agers have been forced to grow spiritually without much help from their churches. I used to go to church with so many questions —Who I am? How do I get in contact with God? How do I go about praying? What is the purpose of my life? How do I meet my problems? I'd sit there in a worship service or a church school class, being taught some doctrine or ethical position, and I'd keep saying to myself, 'What has this got to do with me? When are you going to answer my questions?' But no one did, even when I asked—like it wasn't in the book—so I just got more and more uptight and angry.

"I'm going to admit something to you. Somehow all the time that I'd been sitting around feeling sorry for myself, I really knew—call it instinct or something—that if I could just look through the surface things of my life I would see Christ. Maybe that sounds sort of weird, but I know he is the key to everything. Maybe I should call him God or Holy Spirit instead of Christ. Anyway, you know what I mean—it's that spiritual presence. Don't get the wrong idea—I'm not against the church. It's just that for years I've been looking for something, and not finding it where

I was looking. Now I realize that if the church can't help me, it isn't the end of the search, it's just the beginning.

"So now I'm turning more directly to Christ and making new discoveries about who I am, how to pray, and most of all how to look at life—and it's beautiful! And you know, others are doing the same thing all over the country. In a way, we're doing what we didn't think we could do."

I started to say something in defense of the church, but she was already pointing to a gray stone building.

"Here's where you're supposed to be." With that she handed me a flower and vanished as abruptly as she had appeared.

As I walked on, I could not help thinking of something the anthropologist Loren Eiseley once wrote about being awakened in a forest glade that seemed to him like a sunlit cathedral. A sleek black raven had swooped down to pillage a nest and devour the young of a much smaller bird family. As the raven did what ravens are known to do, a chorus of complaint was lifted not only by the birds under attack but also by a number of other bird families who let their presence be known. All at once everything changed:

. . . then I saw the judgment. It was the judgment of life against death. I will never see it again so forcefully presented. I will never hear it again in notes so tragically prolonged. For in the midst of protest, they forgot the violence. There, in that clearing, the crystal note of a song sparrow lifted hesitantly in the hush. And finally, after painful fluttering, another took the song, and then another. . . . Till suddenly they took heart and sang from many throats joyously together as birds are known to sing. They sang because life is sweet and sunlight beautiful. They sang under the brooding shadow of the raven. In simple truth they had forgotten the raven, for they were the singers of life, and not of death.[1]

No one can deny that the new age drama is not without its brooding shadows. But there is light, and this light is a judgment against the dark . . . any dark.

I scarcely remember addressing the campus group that afternoon, and I don't have any recollection of the plane ride home. My mind was preoccupied with the new age girl and what she had said. Little did I realize that for the next several months I would continue searching out the truth in her words.

One day I was pondering the reference she had made to Christ as the key to life. Actually I could not see anything particularly new or revolutionary in that concept. It is one of the central faith elements of practically all orthodox Christians. It is commonly held that the key Jesus had to give mankind and the one he offered Peter[2] is the key that will unlock a heaven hereafter. Throughout my life I have heard preachers and religious teachers speak of this key almost exclusively in a post-mortem sense. They have said, "If you accept Jesus Christ as your Savior and Lord, you will go to heaven when you die."

Suddenly it occurred to me that the new age understanding of the key Christ has to offer might differ radically from what has been held to be true in the past. Jesus rarely mentioned the next life as such. There are actually very few references in the Gospel record in which Jesus described life on the other side of the grave. Perhaps that is because

1. Loren Eiseley, *The Immense Journey* (New York: Random House, 1957), p. 175.
2. "I will give unto thee the keys of the kingdom of heaven" (Matt. 16:19, KJV).

he experienced heaven not as a futuristic abstract somewhere out in space, but as a particular awareness of God's presence moment by moment filling his life.

For Jesus, the Father was present-tense reality, and heaven surrounded that reality. For us, the creative challenge is to realize that God's presence in our lives makes it possible for heaven to be our present dwelling place. The Christ Spirit in the life of Jesus that made him what he was is also available to us, and this is the key that opens eternal life now, not just hereafter. We need to realize that while God is infinite presence unbounded by time and space, his Spirit is seeking out a dwelling place in our individual lives right now. No wonder the Apostle Paul would cry out to those Christians who conceived of heaven as a futuristic hope and God as a far-off being, "My little children, with whom I am again in travail until Christ [the God presence] be formed in you" (Gal. 4:19). Perhaps the secret to entering eternal life today hinges on how responsive we are to Christ's growing presence in our lives. New age Christians will be able to make an invaluable contribution by living out the truth of this discovery.

Professor William James of Harvard used to say that each child is born into a "psychic sea" of subconscious influence just as real as the air he breathes or the environment in which he lives. This psychic sea is composed for better or worse of the concepts or thought patterns of his family, friends, and community. But what if the individual's sea of thought is polluted by quarter-truths, half-truths, or untruths (not to mention fear, anxiety, worry, and other negatives)?

I thought of the new age girl and the polluted religious influences on her life. Obviously a new "psychic sea" must be developed, and this is the supreme mission of the new age Christian. He affirms Christ life in the midst of structural death, as he realizes eternal life now. He dares to explore the inner terrain of the spirit, sometimes without chart and compass, but with the confidence that something is leading him to the supreme discovery of his life.

In their explorations, new age Christians should make significant contributions in several areas.

In the first place, I feel confident that new age Christians will inevitably center attention more on what a man *is* rather than what he has failed to be. This positive emphasis will magnify the realization of man's spiritual potential rather than the doctrine of original sin. This was the thinking of Jesus who, knowing what was in man, risked his all on the premise that "God created man in his own image" (John 2:24; Gen. 1:27). If Jesus had not believed this, he would not have chosen the words "he came to himself" to describe the moment of truth in the parable of the prodigal son (Luke 15:17).

It follows that Jesus must have accepted the psalmist's position that man was made a "little less than God" (Ps. 8:5). When he was accused of making himself God (John 10:31–34), he referred his accusers to their own law written in the Psalms: "I say, 'You are gods, sons of the Most High, all of you'" (Ps. 82:6). It is difficult to deny that Jesus saw men in the unique position of possessing, at least in latent form, what Meister Eckhart, the fourteenth-century mystic, referred to as "an agent in my soul which is perfectly sensitive to God." This was well evidenced when he challenged his disciples, who were at best ordinary men, with that blinding, unconditional estimate of their identity and worth: "You are the light of the world" (Matt. 5:14).

Notice he did not say that if they would discipline themselves sufficiently, eventually some light would be acquired. He simply announced, "You are the light." This statement becomes even more astounding when we examine the lives of those he referred to as "light." Peter was a temperamental fisherman of questionable loyalty. James and John were ambitious self-seekers. Thomas was a lagging doubter. Nathanael was too easily satisfied. Philip was unaware of God's presence in Jesus, despite having been with him throughout his ministry. Judas was a calculating betrayer. Andrew was bland, and the rest of the group were something less than the brightest stars on the faith horizon.

Furthermore Jesus would accuse these same men of having "little faith." He would witness their temper tantrum which culminated in a request that he call down fire from heaven on those who did not agree with them. He would hear a distraught father accuse his followers of failure to heal when indeed they should have been able to offer some measure of help. He would observe with sadness that not one of the disciples could remain awake with him, even for an hour, through the blood and sweat of his Gethsemane. Finally in the end, all would desert him. Yet it was to these, who bear some resemblance to each of us, that he affirmed: "You are the light." Knowing full well what was in man of truth and error, he held to the conviction that when men are challenged by the Christ-light of redeeming love they will respond via the reflected light of realization within.

In the second place, I believe the new age Christian will see that belief is actually a recognition and a precondition of the ability of God to work. The limits of God's power to act are set "according to your faith," no more, no less. Our praying either narrows down or opens up, depending on the limitations of our belief. Belief is mainly a product of the subconscious mind. What we have been taught, what we have experienced, what we have taken to be true, all constitute the substance out of which our belief grows.

Recently, my son Donny was having trouble with a subject in school. Since he felt that all the other kids in his class were progressing more rapidly than he, his conclusion was that he was stupid and could not excel in this subject, or in any other. At length he had come to believe, despite his prayers to the contrary, that he was unable to cope . . . hence he could not cope.

One evening I told him about how his subconscious mind works. His eyes grew big as I explained how the interior mind contains a wonderful computer into which he feeds data moment by moment each day of his life. Therefore, what he feeds his computer is precisely what it has to work with in his daily experience. I pointed out that a person becomes like that which he believes himself to be.

"Now, Donny," I said, "though you want to do better in this subject and pray for God's help, the chances are that from what you've been feeding your subconscious computer the answer will continue to be, 'No, I can't do it, I'm stupid.' This is the result of negative subconscious programming."

I suggested that we provide his subconscious computer with some new data, beginning with certain affirmations concerning his proven abilities in a variety of areas, such as accomplishments in other school subjects, his gift for giving and receiving friendship, and his talent in athletics, to name a few.

Then I said, "Donny, do you believe that God is smart?"
He nodded affirmatively.

"Okay, you know that picture at church of Christ standing at a door knocking? Right now that is the way God is knocking at the door of your heart."

I tapped on his chest for emphasis, hoping the subconscious mind would get the signal.

"Donny, will you open your heart's door to God?"
He nodded again.

"So be it—God is in your life at this moment. And if God is there, his smartness is there too . . . right in your computer." My son looked at me for a long time without saying a word, then smiled, closed his eyes, and went to sleep.

The next evening as I came home from work, he met me with all his overwhelming eight-year-old enthusiasm. "Dad, I've got the best secret to tell you!" He led me into his room and closed the door to make sure we were out of hearing range of his older sisters.

"Dad, guess what! In school today I tried to spell Chattaroy [the name of the community in which we live], and the teacher said I made a mistake. So I went back to my desk and talked to my computer about God and being smart, and you know what—I spelled it right!"

I have come to see the working reality of this concept. God can only work in our lives to the degree that our subconscious mind allows it. I have been in the company of people who literally rehearse themselves into limitation. One evening while driving to a ball game, a friend began lecturing me on his philosophy of life. In part I recall his saying, "I've heard you talk about a new age and how unlimited God can be if we only believe it. Well, I see life in a different way. I'm a businessman, and I know what the real world is like. It's dog eat dog. If you're going to get somewhere in this life, you've got to do it yourself. No one is going to do that for you . . . not even God. Why, if I didn't work seventeen hours a day, where would I be? Holding down some dinky little job, drawing a dinky little salary, and coming home early to a dinky little house. I believe in God all right, but God is up there"—he pointed his finger toward the sky— "and I'm down here." And so it will be for this man; "according to his faith," his life shall be precisely as he pictures it.

A third area of exploration for the new age Christian, leads us to consider the topic that now becomes the main theme of this book.

There is little doubt that in the evolutionary scheme, we are moving toward the last frontier for exploration. Through the ages the physical boundaries of life have been under constant assault, with man pushing relentlessly even to the fringe of the preposterous, seeking to conquer and claim all possible sensual experience. Perhaps his insatiable lust for everything within the range of the five senses has robbed him of a sustained sensitivity, except for occasional outbursts of caring love, and clear-eyed aspiration for something beyond the merely physical.

Man's achievement on the intellectual boundary has produced a transcending technological power structure of incredible proportion. But, alas, we recognize that this fantastic monument to his collective genius has an incurable failing. It has an appetite so impossibly voracious that it threatens to devour most of the earth's natural resources and befoul the rest in the image of a Frankenstein monster run amuck. Even now, life on this planet is in jeopardy. The ecological limits of life as we know it are in sight. Pollution and attendant forms of destruction are rampant. The gleaming asphalt-glass-steel city of man could well become a graveyard of magnificent mausoleums.

However, a new frontier is opening, and it is like a light shining in the darkness that refuses to be put out. Many new age Christians are celebrating this light with newly discovered eyes created for such viewing.

From the physical standpoint, it is a generally accepted anthropological fact that men of antiquity were not able to use their physical eyesight with the facility of modern man. According to the scholar Gerald Heard, the ability to see the color blue is of late historical vintage. In ancient times, people living along the Blue Nile River in Africa referred to it as brown—never blue. Aristotle indicated that the rainbow had three colors—red, yellow, and green. Furthermore, many people living in the South Pacific still do not discern the three-dimensional aspect of a motion picture. They see only a flat surface and movement.

We are now entering a new era in the evolution of man's ability to see. The passing of the latest milestone, however, will not be noted on the physical or intellectual side of the development ledger. Perhaps it will simply be noted that at this time in history many people developed a way of viewing life based largely on spiritual insights. This Second Sight is a manner of seeing one's situation—sorrow or joy, limitation or fulfillment, absurdity or relevance—set over against the background of God's universal plan and purpose. St. Paul referred to it as "having the eyes of your hearts enlightened" (Eph. 1:18). This enlightened sight deliberately looks beneath the close-up bits and pieces of surface experience. Second Sight discovers a current of spiritual possibility already at work in all the circumstances of life. Primary sight is often so focused on the fouled-up present moment that it is blind to the presence of God and his purpose in creation. Second Sight deliberately attempts to look through the appearance of things, searching for the presence of the creative inner reality.

Dr. Jack Addington tells a story taken from an apocryphal folk legend. It seems that one day Jesus and his disciples came upon a dog at the side of a road that had been dead for several days and was in an advanced state of smelly putrefaction. The disciples passed by quickly to avoid the stench, but Jesus stopped to hover over the animal and finally commented, "What a fine set of teeth he had." This is Second Sight. When conversation around our family table becomes unnecessarily critical of a person, place, or thing, someone invariably remembers the redemptive Second Sight slogan, "What a fine set of teeth he had."

In his autobiography, a famous newspaperman tells of a time when he feared he was going blind. For several weeks he was intensively examined by several doctors, who could find nothing organically wrong with his eyes. In fact, he appeared to have excellent vision; yet his trouble persisted. At last his physicians made a curious diagnosis. They told him he had the eyes of an outdoors man, used to the sight of a far horizon. His profession, however, required him to focus on small newsprint—something they were not inclined to do, so the optic nerve rebelled, and a psychosomatic chain reaction followed that left him ill. The doctors prescribed a long rest in the country and periodic travel to see the grandest views on which he could feast his eyes—majestic mountains, wide stretching seas, and the sweep of great plains. As one doctor put it, "It will not only help your eyes, but it will also do your soul good."

This is Second Sight! It is the lifting of a man's vision from the appearance of things to the ultimate background against which the events of his life are played. It is the recognition that God is always involved in our lives, prompting us to get a larger view of what he can do through us in whatever experience happens to be ours. Paradoxically, it all begins when we see that nothing in time or space is as important as the present moment. Every one of our "nows" is of eternal significance because each is crammed full of God. Indeed it might be better if we never judged a moment as categorically good or bad. As we stand before the mystery of God's universal purpose, that which we now call good could prove to be an enemy in disguise, and that which we presently refer to as bad might well become an uncalculated blessing.

This Second Sight principle is well illustrated in a fascinating episode found in the Book of Acts. In the aftermath of healing a lame man in Jerusalem and preaching that Jesus was resurrected from the dead, Peter and John were arrested and placed in jail. The next day they were obliged to stand before the Sanhedrin (the rulers of the people) to answer certain questions concerning the "authority" of their ministry. The Sanhedrin tribunal, dismayed by the boldness of the two Galilean fishermen who defended themselves with such articulate ease, ordered that they cease and desist from further preaching and teaching in the name of Jesus.

Most Christians today, no matter how dedicated, would probably have despaired at these happenings. Considering the appearance of things, Peter and John might have brought issue with the Almighty: "Why has God subjected us to these disgusting indignities? Why isn't the way being made straight for us? How can we witness effectively for Christ if we must be treated like common criminals for our faith? What hope is there for our movement without more divine support?"

However we have no record of such complaints being voiced by the apostles. I believe the reason for this is that they were men of Second Sight, and so were their friends who had been waiting for them following the Sanhedrin trial. When at last they were reunited in the upper room of Mary's house, instead of bemoaning the surface situation, they prayed a remarkable Second Sight prayer that oriented their present moment to the eternal:

"Sovereign Lord, who didst make the heaven and the earth and the sea and everything in them . . ." (Acts 4:24).

In these words, the power of God was released through a Second Sight scanning of God's overall creative achievements rather than a preoccupation with the morbid immediacy of the problem bobbing around on the surface level. Their belief in the unlimited potential of God to act in the present as he had in the past caused their spirits to fly upward. In the aftermath of that Second Sight prayer, those in the upper room may have spoken again of the Sanhedrin and the problems of the moment, but now their comments were set over against the perspective of God's power, plan, and purpose which had become a glowing reality due to their enlightened interior sight.

My saddest moments of late have been to stand beside the grave of one who has died to this life without ever having opened his second eyes to what was his to see. Though he may have believed, he never really perceived, and this is like dying with your song still unsung. By contrast, in meditation groups around the country I have witnessed, with a degree of Second Sight, a Christlike peace shining through the faces of the straight and the hip, long-haired and close-cropped, male and female, black and white, affluent and nonaffluent, churched and unchurched, young and old—all striving to look long and go deep into the grandeur of God. As consciousness is lifted to Christ's healing presence, one can experience the warmth and shared love in these gatherings, despite apparent diversity that could check the building of loving relationships.

I recall a young man of strong, almost belligerent, opinion coming to a church worship service after experiencing Second Sight accord through a Christ-centered group. He was given an attendance registration card that asked to what church he belonged. At that time he had no affiliation with an organized congregation, so he wrote, "God's Love." This is Second Sight.

When a person develops Second Sight, his face usually undergoes an interesting metamorphosis. A childlike openness of wonder and curiosity joins with a mature knowing that emerges from a hidden depth of being—joyfully bubbling at times, serenely quiet at others. It is the look of those who are disentangling themselves from a life trampled under by enthroned negativism, who now seek a heightened consciousness of God's presence behind all the scenes of their daily experience. They may discover this uplift in meditative prayer, from penetrative Scripture reading, through the resources of inspirational art, music, and drama. They may be reminded of God by something from a spiritually motivating book, the words of a discerning friend, a human encounter, something seen or heard in the out-of-doors, or the thoughts gathered from a Christ-centered lecture or sermon.

It is not uncommon for those experiencing Second Sight suddenly to begin laughing like Lazarus did in Eugene

O'Neil's play. After Jesus had raised him from the dead, he spent his time softly laughing at the pretenses, rationalizations, and obsessions with externals of the townsfolk in the village of Bethany. Lazarus had seen through into the life eternal and he was intoxicated with the joy of the Spirit. He came to tell the villagers that "there is no death," but he did it with such laughter that it was too much for them. The magnetic look in his eyes drew them like moths to a flame, but they were increasingly afraid of his strange challenge and feared that he was leading them to overstep the bounds of human limitation and belief. With his laughter he was inviting them to discover a deeper life awaiting them within. Finally when they could stand it no longer, they seized him and put him back in the tomb. They sealed it with a rock and believed with all their "old age" hearts that they had at last stilled the troublesome laughter and put an end to the unsettling sight of that recklessly joyful face.

Today, at long last, they are proven wrong. The Lazarus laughter has returned, the Lazarus face has multiplied, the new age has arrived. Now, at last, men will be able to see "face to face" with laughter what was previously seen "in a mirror dimly."

A warning should be sounded for those who seek this Second Sight. Beware of the cultists, ism-ists, drug trippers, out-of-sight visionaries, ego cultivators, and wizardly conmen whose stock-in-trade are the thrills and chills of emotional excitement. Beware of the grandiose promises that by doing their thing one can become a super-person with unlimited power.

After observing some of those other frustrating approaches up close, I can report that Second Sight is a balanced, disciplined effort of personal watchfulness. There is a day-by-day trial-and-error effort to seek the proper rhythm of study, quiet, service, fellowship, work, diet, and exercise. But it is more. There is the willingness to experience mystery, the curiosity to seek deeper meanings, the capacity for wonder, the joy of spontaneity, and the penetration of outward things to discern the impress of God's love and his eternal purpose. When at last something of this is developed in our experience, the blur that obscures so many of life's most profound meanings will recede, and what was hidden will be revealed.

And that's what this book is all about—getting through to what is real via the channel of Second Sight.

## ✳ 2

# YOUTH,
# PRAYER, AND ESP

*"If the church had offered me a way to break through in the Spirit and find myself, drugs would not have been necessary."*

*—A student, aged 20.*

# YOUTH,
# PRAYER, AND ESP

An anxious mother, acting as the spokesman for several silent parents, phoned to request that I meet with the senior high youth group and, in her words, "teach them to pray and get closer to God." She nervously advised me that our kids were "losing interest in religion" and it was "my duty to make Christians out of them!" Grinding teeth always set me on edge, and hers were.

I suppose I could have fenced with her on what she meant by "prayer," "getting closer to God," "religion," and even what it is to be a Christian—but it was 11:00 P.M. I was weary and knew that even if we talked all night we wouldn't get much beyond religious words and slogans. One good thing though—at least she wasn't ordering up another lecture on sex or pot. In the strained silence that drifted between us, I wondered what on earth I could say to the kids in this command performance that I had not said before in church, youth groups, or elsewhere. Frankly I was sick of saying the same old things and forever being someone's religious mouthpiece. I agreed to her proposed meeting with all the enthusiasm I used to generate late at night when a police sergeant

would phone for me to drive down to the drunk tank and
bring home a church member.

On a Wednesday evening the group arrived one by one,
heads lowered, following each other like driven cattle. We
gathered in my first floor study at the church and exchanged
cautious greetings. There was an unsuccessful attempt at
conversation—someone laughed—then all was quiet. Now I
was expected to speak. After all that's the way it was supposed to be—me speaking, them listening. I resented this
contrived encounter and desperately wanted to tell the group
how I really felt, but their parents were still paying my
salary. At that moment I wasn't quite ready to become a
starving new age revolutionary. We sat there looking at each
other. The wind-up clock on my desk never ticked louder or
called more attention to itself. A dark-haired sophomore
glanced at the clock, then at his girlfriend. Unfortunately I
could read his thoughts.

Finally I began talking in uninspired generalities about
prayer, the Christian life, and serving one's fellow-man.
Speaking to groups has always been easy for me, particularly
with the young, but this was different. I was almost tongue-
tied. I kept looking for some communication lever like an
engaging story or a group participation gimmick . . . anything to win approval and stimulate interest. After twenty
minutes or so of winging it alone, I asked for discussion—
hoping against hope to get into genuine dialogue. No one
spoke for what seemed like a week.

Then a two-hundred-pound athlete with a sharp incisive
mind leaned forward and with cold, brutal logic challenged
me: "If you can prove the power of the invisible, then maybe
I'll accept what you say about prayer, Christ, and all that

spiritual stuff. If you can't, then there isn't much point in my coming back."

A dozen heads nodded in agreement.

How could anyone prove such a thing? I tried to make light of the challenge, pointing to the absurdity of such an undertaking. "You're putting me on," I laughed, falling back in my chair with my eyes closed. But when I reopened them, there wasn't the slightest trace of a responding smile or expression of accommodation in the whole room. Each face was set with a no-nonsense singleness of purpose. Incredibly, I was actually on trial, with these kids as my judge and jury. I asked for a week to think it over and try to research an answer. Frankly, I was surprised that the group consented so readily.

With seven days allowed for unlocking the secret of invisible power, I searched like a mad man for any clue to the proof I needed. I visited several libraries, read stacks of books and magazines, asked friends for assistance, sought information from out-of-town sources. Nothing seemed to help. In fact the goal became more elusive than ever. My distress and helplessness increased with each passing day.

On the third night of that awful week I had an unsettling nightmare. I dreamed I was the catcher from Salinger's book *The Catcher in the Rye*. Because I could not catch the kids before they jumped over the cliff, I was replaced by another catcher. Awakening in a cold sweat, panicked by the symbolism in the dream, I realized that if I failed to prove the invisible to this high school group, I would surely lose not only my ministry to them, but God knows what else.

On the afternoon of the seventh day, three hours before the showdown meeting, I decided it was time to turn this bad scene completely over to the Lord. Had I known about the perspective of Second Sight, I could have been delivered from a week of torture. After a few moments of meditation, I began to see the situation in terms of God's ability to answer his creature's need. This was the background orientation I needed.

Despite the fact that time was running out I felt a sudden release from anxiety, and for some unexplainable reason I opened a book of parlor games that had been on my bookshelf for several years. The title of one chapter leaped off the page, "Extrasensory Perception Entertainment for All the Family." The subtitle read, "An Adventure in Proving the Power of the Invisible Mind." I could scarcely believe my eyes. I can't remember ever being more elated.

The young people arrived like a tribe of happy minstrels thirty minutes before the scheduled meeting time—in marked contrast to our first meeting. They were in high spirits, racing up and down the church corridors, playfully throwing themselves against my study door. Actually, I believe they were hopeful that I would come up with something to meet their challenge, and so was I.

The evening's activities began with my passing out paper and pencils as suggested in the ESP (extrasensory perception) chapter of the game book. Next I shuffled homemade cards and placed them face down on a table within eyesight of everyone in the room. The underside of each card was marked with the traditional ESP symbols (from Dr. Rhine's work at Duke University)—a square, wavy lines, star, circle, and plus sign. I requested that all concentrate and try to perceive the identity of each card in the order of its appearance on the table. The experiment was repeated six times. Three times I was aware of the card sequence and attempted telepathically to communicate it to the group. The results were dismally inconclusive, but the young people appeared stimulated by the novelty of the experiment and, perhaps more important, by the fact that I was attempting to be relevant.

Next, we tried a game called "Color Sending." One person leaves the room while the remaining group fastens its attention on a primary color and attempts to project it via a telepathic wavelength to the receiver outside the room. We visualized the person receiving the transmission completely covered with the color sent. Much to my chagrin the person who volunteered as our first receiver was a girl of very limited mental capacity, generally regarded by her peers as "the dumbest girl in school." I cringed as the door closed behind her. It seemed inconceivable that she would receive anything. After twenty minutes of experimentation we were struck dumb with amazement. Our volunteer was sent eleven colors, and she received them all without a miss. This sensational demonstration not only gave each of us an unforgettable experience, but it also propelled her into a realm of accomplishment which she would have never dared to dream about. Several others also scored well on this experiment.

The highlight of the evening, at least for me, came when the athlete who had started the hassle in the first place exclaimed, "Man, I'm a believer." I breathed a prayer of thanksgiving.

In our next meetings we included, along with color sending, more difficult exercises, such as the transmission of numbers, words, and objects. In all cases we used the same general principles of sending and receiving. We would see the number, word, or object in our own minds and then visualize it etched on the forehead of the one receiving. This effort of undistracted focusing was very difficult at first, mainly because we had not taken the necessary steps for tuning in.

As the weeks rolled by, members of the group developed a deeper understanding of how extrasensory perception works, but more important we were learning the basic fundamentals for employing the awareness faculty we began to call Second Sight. Early in our research we established a premise that became tremendously helpful in future efforts—focusing attention is an essential consideration for all invisible power activity, whether it be in the elementary stages of transmitting telepathic messages man to man or the higher spiritual level of God-man communication.

In one of our focusing exercises, I would hold a pencil before the experimenters for approximately ten seconds. Then each person would be requested to reproduce on paper the pencil that had been placed before them. The group always marveled at how little they had actually seen of the pencil—even in ten seconds. The exercise would be repeated as many as six times before the pencil was fully viewed by the group members. This particular routine and others similar to it were used at the beginning of each meeting for nearly a year.

Recognizing the need for greater physical control in our experimenting, we spent considerable time learning to relax our bodies by commanding the body parts to be passive—such as closing the eyes, relaxing the face muscles, unclenching the teeth, letting the jaw go slack, breathing rhythmically, and ordering the major body muscles to be relaxed from head to toe. Sometimes we would practice the Yoga method of tensing each body part from feet to head on command and then completing the cycle by relaxing the body parts in isolation, all the time keeping the rest of one's physical being in tension. In this exercise we would start with the head and move downward. The state of relaxation that follows this exercise is a beautiful feeling of limpness. The best posture for this activity is to lie flat on the back or sit with the back against a wall.

Learning to breathe deeply and rhythmically is another factor in the process of "tuning in." Most people use very little of their total lung capacity in breathing. When several minutes are devoted to the process of a deep steady intake of air (as the yogis teach), with the mouth slightly open forming the word "hong," and on the exhale of breath forming the word "saw," a further sense of interior alertness and peace is experienced. Awareness sensitivity is increased tremendously by focusing, relaxing, and deep breathing.

Following this, we experimented with concentrating on the screen of the mind, which we visualized inwardly as a white movie screen. This was our first attempt at deliberately opening a dimension of Second Sight. The doubts of the past concerning the validity of ESP were now behind us. The preliminary exercises of body control and concentration had served to whet our appetites for deeper adventure.

One evening I asked the group to gather in a circle with paper and pencil. We went through our focusing, relaxation, breathing exercises, and then I asked that each person search the screen of his mind as I called the first name of each person around the circle. Three minutes were allowed for group concentration on whatever activities, environmental responses, thoughts and feelings that the person named might have experienced throughout the previous day. I suggested that we attempt to visualize via a time tunnel regression—to live a few moments in another person's past. Since most of

the people involved were in school together, they were
obliged to cancel out remembrances of that which might
have been consciously seen and heard. I allowed approximately a minute for recording impressions before calling the
name of the next person in the circle.

When the results were read at the close of the session, oh's
and ah's and other expressions of delight filled the room. It
was not uncommon to hear accurate descriptions of what a
person had eaten for supper, exact details of a room or house
never seen, the emotional response of a person involved in
some activity unknown to the experimenters, or the color of
a subject's new dress, shirt, or tie not yet worn in public.

One evening I suggested that we experiment with Sir
Francis Bacon's much-discussed concept of the human aura.
This is one of the least-known but most intriguing subjects
of investigation for a discovery group. Scientists tell us that
all living things give off vibrations, and under certain conditions these are observable. We found that almost anyone
(including the rank beginner), with even a molecule of
concentration, can usually see a radiance outlining the head
and body of another person if he is in a dimly lighted room
looking at someone against a pastel colored surface. The conditions I have suggested create an ideal viewing situation;
however, auras can be seen under far less perfect circumstances by the more experienced in this field of research.
Many people have been seeing auras all their lives and have
thought it only a blurring of the eyesight or an optical illu-
sion.

It is amazing how nearly everyone will see the halo light
encircling another person the first time they try. Some even
observe a variety of colors in the aura. Comments from a
typical group watching a person's aura are:

"I can see it over his head."

"There it is."

"Now it's to the right."

"Yes, I can see it now—to the right and down the arm."

"I can see it too."

"So can I. It's incredible!"

"This is fantastic! Look, you can see a light—it looks like a halo."

"Now it's on the left."

At times one can see colors in the aura that range the whole spectrum.

I am now convinced that the paintings of the saints that include the inevitable halo were the result of the artists' actually seeing the auras of spiritually alive persons. Indeed it would have been a serious error in judgment, and a tragic loss to posterity, for an artist to subtract whatever perception he had of the person he was painting. We can be thankful for the spiritual and artistic honesty of those "aware" masters of the past.

Another experiment I have used with various groups is to place a sending group in one room and a receiving group in another, both equipped with chalk and chalkboards. The senders write a word, draw a symbol, or sketch a face, and telepathically transmit that image to the receiving group, who in turn attempt to reproduce what they have received on their chalkboard. This can be a fascinating activity depending on the intensity of concentration.

One Sunday evening at a senior high gathering, I asked that a boy (who seemed to have unusual transmitting ability) take a chalkboard to the third floor of the building. Next I asked two girls with good receiving and sending ability to take their position beside a chalkboard on the second floor.

The rest of us gathered on the main floor before our chalk-board. I signaled for the third floor occupant to draw one of the five ESP symbols on his board and transmit it to the second floor. The girls were directed to place the symbol received on the board and transmit it down to us and we would collectively decide what to put on the board. Two out of three times we had the same string of circles and stars on the three chalkboards!

As the word spread of our activities, we were frequently invaded by curiosity seekers who wanted to know what was going on. The presence of newcomers to the group meetings had not the slightest element of distraction. In fact the group enjoyed the challenge of testing their extrasensory perception on new persons and watching them come alive with a positive desire to develop their own spiritual gifts.

During these days I was wrestling inwardly with the problem of which way we were going as a group. Could I spiritually justify the weird experiences we were having? For instance, hearing someone who was not at my dinner table describe the lettuce salad I had enjoyed at supper; sitting with a group of teenagers observing the halo aura around someone's head; witnessing telepathic communication so startling even the skeptics and doubters would admit to the truth of it.

My training in systematic theology with all its Aristotelian thought forms and a lifetime orthodox church background haunted all the unsystematic, nontraditional, anti-Aristotelian research in which I was engaged. I felt like an overgrown clown playing games that served no more important purpose than to satisfy the craving kids have for novelty. What had any of this to do with spiritual development?

One day a friend, who is a student of the occult, informed

me that my experimentation with the young people was helping them "unfold their psychic awareness." I must confess that comment did not exactly put my mind at ease. Although I have good friends in that field, I still regard much of their activity as a hang-up. I have known a few "psychic freaks" who spend their lives consorting with low spirits of undetermined origin, who never break out into the wider experience of the Christ-centered spiritual heights. I kept praying for guidance, asking that we follow the leading of Christ in all our efforts and that the ministering angels attend us at every turn.

One evening a serious-minded girl asked me, "What have these experiments to do with Christ?" Little did she realize that this was a crisis question. She had touched an exposed nerve. I prayed inwardly for an appropriate response, seeking a Second Sight perspective. Suddenly, with an inbreak of revelation, I was able to answer not only her question but my own as well. I told her that I considered Christ to be, among other things, the supreme, living, personal, communicating Spirit who remains invisible to our outward eyes but is nonetheless real to the inward sight. I went on to say that until that time we had been attempting to establish the reality principle of invisible power for those having trouble with this concept. But now I felt the group was ready to move toward a deeper experience of the inward Christ.

She seemed satisfied with this explanation, and for the time being I felt the blessing of an untroubled conscience. However from that time on we always prefaced our experimentive activities with the prayer, "Christ, please give us awareness of what you want us to see that will be of service to you, and may our experiments be in tune with your overall plan for us."

On another occasion a concerned church woman asked me
if the Old Testament (Deut. 18:9–14) did not give explicit
orders forbidding us from having anything to do with the
likes of ESP. My answer to her and others with the same
problem is that extra (beyond the ordinary) sensory (having
to do with the senses) perception (awareness) is a neutral
power built into each person as a gift from God. If ESP can
help open the door of one's Second Sight to seek the universal
truth of God's presence and purpose, then I cannot help but
see it as a profound blessing. Obviously ESP can be employed for good or evil. It is possible for one to misuse his
gift and become a self-serving dabbler in witchcraft, or he
can use the same gift to tap the mysteries of the heavenly
world and release a creative flow of spiritual impressions to
serve the good of man.

For instance, in one situation Peter, James, and John in
heightened consciousness exercised their extra-sense perception—their Second Sight—when they saw Jesus transfigured.
". . . and his face shone like the sun and his garments became white as light. And behold, there appeared to them
Moses and Elijah, talking with him" (Matt. 17:2–3). The
ESP–Second Sight faculty was employed for the highest
purposes when Zechariah saw an angel, when the shepherds
on a hillside saw the Christmas angels, when Joseph and
Mary received an angelic visitation; when Elijah, Gideon,
Jacob, David, Moses, Joshua—to name a few—were visited
by angels. The Bible is filled with the stories of supernatural
signs and wonders seen by tuned in people. It is a document
of miraculous happenings occurring to people of Second
Sight, the testimony of men and women who have used their
extrasensory perception, a dimension of Second Sight awareness, for the highest purposes. Jesus said to those who would

follow in his path, "He who believes in me will also do the works that I do; and greater works than these will he do, because I go to the Father" (John 14:12).

My answer to the concerned woman who questioned the "propriety" of developing the ESP gift is simply what Jesus suggested as an acid test for all the issues of life, "Thus you will know them by their fruits" (Matt. 7:20). If a person exercising his extrasensory perception (Second Sight) is meeting the challenges of life in a creative, redemptive way and is serving the cause of Christ, what more needs to be proved or explained? The crucial need for people today is to be immersed in the reality of God's limitless universal concern for their personal lives, which includes the support of the heavenly hosts—and all are as available to each of us as in the days of the biblical record.

One evening a girl on the brink of tears, fumbling in the darkness of a personal problem, told us about her father's hospitalization and of the terrible pain he was suffering. She said that his illness had not as yet been officially diagnosed, but the doctors were working around the clock for an answer. Immediately we went into Second Sight visualization, scanning the screen of our minds, seeking the mind of Christ, and centering on the largest picture of wholeness we could see. The results were amazingly helpful as the universal was particularized. One boy saw that the pain would be relieved if the father's bed were raised and his legs elevated. Another boy discerned that he was suffering from some sort of blood disease. Two others pictured the need for more water in the father's diet and a program of physical exercise with a restricted diet.

When the girl arrived at the hospital, equipped with her Second Sight data, she began making suggestions at once.

First she asked the nurse on duty to raise the lower part of her father's bed. The nurse was not about to do anything until she checked her chart. Then she blushed a bright crimson—the order to have the bed raised had been issued the previous evening but for some reason had been overlooked. When the father's legs were in the new position, his pain subsided almost immediately. Within a few days the sickness was diagnosed as a rare blood disease, and he was placed on a restricted diet that included large amounts of water.

On another occasion, a boy was warned while in reflection not to go home by the same route he had taken earlier in the evening. In our meditation time he had visualized a high speed automobile accident involving several cars. Fortunately he followed his guidance, because that very evening there was a terrible automobile collision involving four cars with two people killed on the exact route and at the same time he would have been traveling home.

These were among the first of our predictive reflections— but not the last. We had to learn how to record the messages mentally and simply wait to see what would develop without mobilizing anxiety. Occasionally people were helped by the futuristic material, but in most cases the prophecies were so general that they were difficult to analyze for specific guidance.

Eventually we launched experiments in intercessory prayer for people known to have physical, mental, or spiritual need. With the spiritual reality principle now firmly established in the leading of Christ, we were ready as a group to send out our prayers confidently on behalf of others. Frankly I had been looking forward to this "serving ministry" for a long time. When praying for a person's wholeness, we visualized the one in need as being immersed in the white and golden light of Christ's healing power. It would be like seeing a person enveloped in a luminous aura, cleansing and purifying his whole being. We would hold this picture in close concentration, seeking God's perfect universal will to be done. Our prayer efforts were generally followed by checking on the results, which gave all involved an increased sense of mission in the prayer projects. Eventually people of various age groups from other churches began to ask our group to pray for a variety of needs. Each time this happened the kids took it in stride, but I felt a terrific sense of exaltation —we were really serving someone besides ourselves. When I said so, a group member reflected, "Welcome to the new age."

After a few months of this spiritual research, the parents of the group members seemed happy if not mystified by the changes that had transpired in the lives of their sons and daughters. Notwithstanding the reservations they may have had concerning our unorthodox methods, they were at least impressed by the living results. One mother who had been unusually anxious about her son's spiritual condition, complained vaguely, "My son has really changed. He prays about everything, talks about Second Sight, and almost embarrasses us by his comments on the power of God. If we're not careful, he's going to end up being a minister"—as if that was the worst thing she could imagine.

While traveling to a youth retreat in the Middle West, it occurred to me that tuning in for Second Sight through relaxation, focusing, visualizing the screen of the mind, and seeking Christ's guidance to serve the will of God was actually a process of meditation which could be defined as the manward preparation to receive. When, after this prepara-

tion, one begins to experience something coming from another direction over which he has no direct control, at that
moment he is in the highest sense involved in contemplative
awareness that many of us have come to believe is God-given.

The next day I presented this theory to the retreat and laid
out the steps of meditation procedure more deliberately than
was my custom when leading a short-term group experience.
After several hours of preparation, I asked the young people
to find a place to be alone and meditate on the name "Christ"
for the purpose of receiving what God had to give them in
contemplation. Thirty minutes later the group reassembled,
and the reflective insights were remarkable.

One boy (a senior in high school) recorded:

> Christ is Spirit, the Spirit that moves the universe. Christ
> who was fully seen in Jesus is in me, and I am growing in
> awareness of His being there. He is my life. For me to live
> is Christ. Christ is life. From time to time I actually see
> Him, though not like I see other things. . . . Like when I
> have helped someone I see Him in that person's face. I have
> come to the conclusion there is nothing else but Him.

A girl (junior in high school) wrote:

> Christ is not some far-off heavenly symbol. He is in the
> blood, sweat and tears of my life. Because He comes to me
> with love, I feel His love through me for others. The goal of
> Christ in me is to bring harmony within and help extend it
> through the world.

Through the medium of Second Sight experiments, such as
these, a genuine spiritual happening can take place.

A thorny problem occasionally emerges following one of
our Second Sight retreats. When a young person tells his
parents or minister (if they are tradition-bound with closed

minds to spiritual innovation) about his ESP–Second Sight development, he should be prepared for an explosion of denunciation. I urge the young people simply to explain their desire to prepare themselves to receive the gifts of the Spirit and to say that they are seeking Christ's guidance in the most realistic way they can. Then they should love those giving them a hard time . . . and go right on with their ESP–Second Sight development. And in the words of one young Second Sighter, "This way is better than being bored by dull Youth Fellowship programs that no one understands or cares about, singing 'Kum Ba Yah,' and trying to pinch each other."

During a conference with a southern church, I had five evenings with the senior high youth group. After a session or two of orientation, I wrote some quotations on the chalkboard, one of which was taken from contemporary literature. The experimenters were to go off alone for fifteen minutes of focused reflection, seeking an interpretation to what had been placed before them. The results were significant. In one experiment, I wrote on the board, with no identification, the frequently quoted words from Jean-Paul Sartre's play *No Exit*, "Hell is other people." While none of the young people had seen the play or read it, nearly all visualized the play as taking place in a single room. Several were aware of people talking about something very unpleasant. Two recognized that one character in the play was reacting to the evil in other people with him. Another recognized that the setting for the play was hell. I do not attempt to explain this—just record it!

Marshall McLuhan, the controversial professor, has suggested that the "Gutenberg era" of reliance on the printed word is coming to an end and today the medium is the message. The Christian enterprise should take note of this. The

medium of research through first-hand experiments with
the invisible power can stimulate a sense of vitality and
aliveness. We need desperately to explode the idea that
spiritual reality is to be measured by saying the right religious
words, involving ourselves in the right church structures, and
following the paths of unquestioned tradition. We must remember that the medium is the message and a Christ experience can take place out of a spontaneous Second Sight
happening.

One afternoon I was speaking on the subject of ESP–
Second Sight at a PTA meeting. In a question-answer period
following the talk, a thoughtful woman asked, "Have you
ever tried these experiments with adults? I think we need it
as much as our kids." She was right of course. That is why
there are so many spiritual life groups springing up across
America, in and out of the church. But let me post a warning.
If a group, no matter how dedicated, relies too much on form
and tradition—theories and words about the spiritual life—
and fails to probe below the surface to discover a Second
Sight dimension, that group is in danger of becoming like the
many contemporary churches that rely almost entirely on
verbal expression instead of spiritual happening.

Another woman in the same group asked if any of our
experimenters in Second Sight development have been on
drugs. My answer was in the affirmative. In all honesty some
of them have taken drugs either out of curiosity or because
they were seeking a spiritual breakthrough. Many have
reasoned that a drug experience would help them attain an
advanced state of understanding and exhilarating release
from the restricting patterns of common life.

The way of Second Sight, however, requires a total effort
of body, mind, and spirit to achieve the deeper level of con-

sciousness in which one becomes aware in every part of his being of his relationship to the whole of life. It is easy to disregard the fact that when one tampers with the realities of his life through the use of drugs, he is undercutting his ability to meet the challenges of his environment, which can be self-destructive. Drugs have a tendency to mobilize feelings only on spectacular peaks of exhilaration. Only a small portion of one's being arrives at those high experience levels, while the spiritual grasp of cosmic relationships trails behind. Second Sight is a unified experience of ever-increasing awareness, because it gives the total man communion with God without the restrictions of an artificial channel that is doing him psychological and physiological damage. Those on drugs achieve, at most, a partial realization of something beyond themselves, but by Second Sight standards this is not sufficient.

In some of our groups it is interesting to note the drug users with their dull eyes, suspended animation reflexes, and far-away expressions. Eventually they want to know what the group is experiencing that they are not; when they come prepared for the allness of our experimentation, it means they are no longer "takers."

I recall some mystical moments spent with one of the formerly messed up young men in our original group, following the death of his father. He had gone the route of sensation seeking in the outward experience, but eventually found his inward path to the source of life. In the day following the father's sudden passing, I went to visit the family that included the young man and his mother. I shall not forget the three hours we spent conversing on the meaning of eternal life. Rarely have I seen two people so moved by a discussion of spiritual awareness and the wonderful world to come. Their eyes glowed, smiles appeared, even laughter broke out, much to the consternation of a passing parade of mourners.

Then I began to experience the strangest sensation. We seemed to be surrounded by the presence of what the Book of Hebrews calls "a host of witnesses." By the will of a fantastic purpose beyond our own, we found ourselves in the presence of angels just as surely as it is described in the biblical stories. The vibrations in the room were so powerful I nearly lost my breath. Faint golden hues moved about us. I felt a surge of uplifting energy and revitalizing power. Friends of the family arrived in a steady stream bringing food, groping for expressions of condolence, shedding sympathetic tears. They were scarcely noticed, not because we wished to be impolite, it was just that our hearts burned with an unspeakable joy which nothing could diminish. We knew beyond any shadow of doubt that there is no death—just Christ . . . love . . . peace . . . light and LIFE . . . LIFE . . . *LIFE*.

My description of what happened on that memorable afternoon when three people in a contemporary setting were entertained by angels may upset a few readers! All I can say is that we simply lifted our eyes to the greatness of God, who invites us to utilize the gift of Second Sight, to make our own discoveries, to enter the new age and experience what the biblical writers call "signs and wonders." This is what the young in spirit are doing.

I cannot speak with an absolute word concerning what the gift of Second Sight may mean to those who cultivate it. Casting one's life against the reality of God (who is, as the song goes, "big enough to rule His mighty universe but small enough to live within the heart"), and seeing beneath the surface of a given life situation may prove to be the common experience of those who have entered the new age as "new" people of the Spirit. They will only be employing what God has made available to them. Indeed all men in this new age are being called by the same Voice: "Open your eyes and see with the faculty of that which has been unknown—and let your whole body be filled with a light never dreamed possible."

I am very much aware that what I am talking about must be experienced before it can have even a semblance of reality. I remember hearing about a gifted woman professor who had the reputation of being an outstanding scholar in the field of English literature. In a discussion of the poetry of Elizabeth Barrett Browning, she admitted that while she appreciated the meaning of the words, Mrs. Browning's love sonnets simply did not awaken any responding sense of reality in her. Several people expressed amazement that she, a highly regarded student of literature and an outstanding teacher and critic, could not see the beauty that seemed so obvious to them. Not all wondered, however. A few knew why she had missed the sight of such beauty—she had never been in love, certainly not as Mrs. Browning had been.

Experience is essential. So I invite you into the arena of participation where you may test the truth of what is recorded here. Then you will know—not believe or disbelieve that such things are possible, but *know*.

■3

# WHEN
# LIFE TUMBLES IN

*A minister friend told me how his church caught fire and burned to the ground in less than an hour. Later he stood weeping in the smoldering debris. There was nothing left, nothing at all. Even his pulpit was destroyed. But his eyes caught sight of something in the black embers, something the fire had not destroyed. He picked it up and shook off the clinging ashes. It was a wisp of paper from the liturgy he had read the previous Sunday. He read it aloud there in that devastated place: "I believe in God the Father Almighty, Maker of heaven and earth." God was there. He felt the surge of new life. God was there where life had tumbled in. All this must be attributed to the man's Second Sight.*

# 3

# WHEN
# LIFE TUMBLES IN

For twelve years I was minister of a church that had grown structurally from a little village chapel by the side of the road to a rambling suburban edifice whose reputation, largely exaggerated, for being a spiritual life center had become far reaching. Through the early years of my pastorate, no one could have enjoyed a more free-wheeling, lively ministry than was mine while in the confines of a denominational structure. Perhaps this was because most of our congregation paid little if any attention to the fact that we were a church with a brand name. We simply did not have the accepted appetite for "mother church" participation that seemed unrelated to our immediate situation. We were attempting to live out a style of church life unfettered by headquarters' regulations or bureaucratic direction, and to express our Christian response as we felt spiritually motivated—which was fun while it lasted.

However as our church grew in size and influence, the pressures toward organizational uniformity grew proportionately. The problem, simply put, is that from an administrative point of view our involvement in such activities as spiritual life groups, experimentation in prayer techniques, prayer chains, prayer vigils, disciplined living for Christ, healing therapy, ESP–Second Sight development, investigation into the reality of immortality and examination of Eastern religions' approach to spiritual attainment were looked on with something less than enthusiasm. Since these investigative pursuits did not fall into convenient categories of statistical analysis, they were considered suspect. All this, coupled with my failure to attend what I considered to be time-wasting meetings, lent credence to the indictment that I was not a good company man.

A certain dyed-in-the-wool denominational executive invited me to lunch and attempted to intimidate me over chicken salad concerning my future in the church. If I did not start attending more of his ministers' gatherings, he told me sternly, he would report this to my episcopal leader, and my future success (meaning a larger church) would be in jeopardy.

I will not report my part of that conversation because I really didn't say much of anything. Fumbling without a Second Sight perspective, I saw my future in the hands of this threatening person across the table, and I was scared. I have long since regretted my shameful silence. If only I had looked that man in the eye and said, "Knock it off." But I didn't, and we are both poorer for my lapse. I am now convinced that I was only able to serve such a comparatively long ministerial hitch because our church regularly paid its financial assessments and always received well over a hundred new members each year.

The serious rumbles did not really begin, however, until another denominational official confided to a leader of our church that for some time he had been "covering up" for me, and that other ministers in our district were taking up my share of the "organizational burden" (a precise definition) so that I could be a free spirit. A climax of sorts was reached when I accepted an invitation to visit a minister friend in another part of the country to discuss the possibility of my succeeding him at his retirement. This conversation took place without the knowledge and consent of my "superiors" and was judged a flagrant violation of protocol. According to what I assume must be some special in-rule of social amenities, the "proper" thing would have been for me to inform certain high-ranking denominational officials that I had been invited to the interview, in order to receive their permission or blessing or something. The only problem is that I had no knowledge of such a rule and, for that matter, I did not know ahead of time what would be discussed at the meeting with the minister friend. If this sounds confusing, please remember I am writing several months later with the clarifying (?) perspective of time. This unpleasant misadventure simply accentuated my growing need to break out of what had become a suffocating space of existence.

If, however, I have mistakenly conveyed the impression that those set over against me were all wrong and I was perfectly right, then I have committed a gross error. I have not forgotten Chekhov's comment, "You will not become a saint through other people's sin."

I cannot remember precisely when that wild, illogical, Second Sight idea began to blow against my mind, but I actually saw myself on a sabbatical leave. I visualized a time of perfect peace and spiritual recovery in which I could take long walks hand in hand with my wife, play with the chil-

dren, wear old clothes, grow a beard, repolish some tarnished
truths more or less taken for granted, and spend long hours in
spiritual renewal.

At first this crazy "stop the world" notion was nothing
more than a wishful impulse, a delightful escape mechanism
—a lovely fantasy. Crazy idea or not, something had to be
done! God was shouting at me through the language of
events, and alternately I attempted to focus, relax, and scan
the screen of my mind for a guidance picture. But the appearance of external things was so dominant I could not see
the spiritual reality. I was blinded by my belief in what
seemed to be impossibly negative factors. For two weeks I
paced the floor asking myself whether or not I should take a
sabbatical. Even the question seemed preposterous. How
could a thirty-seven-year-old minister with a wife and three
children cut himself off from a position of financial security
and seniority status?

In comic opera fashion our situation was further compli-
cated when I was asked to accept a singularly unchallenging
church assignment that offered nothing more than a larger
salary and "a fine parsonage." Sweet reasonableness suggested that by a show of dogged determination I could remain in my pastorate for another year, but the thought of
just hanging on for any length of time offered all the appeal
of a wilderness trail going nowhere.

The days of my dilemma seemed endless and the nights
were even worse. The truth of Nietzsche's words were in-
carnated in my dilemma: "Gaze not too deeply into the
abyss, lest the abyss gaze into you." That is precisely what
was happening. The time for making a decision was at hand,
but I was still without positive guidance. I prayed for some
Second Sight light of understanding, but no light was given.

I prayed for the solid ground of assurance, but no such ground was provided. I prayed for someone to give me an answer, but no answer was forthcoming. In the midst of all this, I spent two weeks suffering from an emotionally induced sinus attack that only made the decision-making predicament worse. A stuffy head does not groove one in the direction of awareness.

So what good was my religious faith and Second Sight experience when I needed it most? How relevant were those cherished spiritual truths, when my life was tumbling in? I was stumbling down stupidity street, when all around were the evidences of what I needed to see but did not see. Imperceptibly, though, the very thing I needed most was being given—God was granting me the grace of endurance. I should have been more aware. He let me fumble about in the darkness, perhaps for the sake of ego need that agonizes and dramatizes the human crisis. Miraculously, by some measure of unfamiliar patience, I kept moving forward . . . to wait it out . . . to stay on my feet.

No small help came from my positive, Second-Sightful, understanding wife—who kept reassuring me that God's perfect will would be done. She was the calm of my storm. Her Second Sight was not the least bit dimmed by the outward circumstance.

In a lighter vein, one evening after an intensive time of spiritual seeking, the sewage system backed up in the parsonage basement. Later that night our oldest daughter claimed she had seen a ghost in her closet. I interpreted these events as a sure sign to take the sabbatical. Seriously, and I do mean seriously, within the space of a single week, through a windfall of fortuitous happenings, a string of lucrative speaking engagements opened up—like a miracle—and the

impractical sabbatical dream suddenly became a realistic
financial possibility.

At last the decision could be made. I thanked the Lord and
sent a letter of resignation off to headquarters with a measure
of relief—and I must add a sense of unreality. Then on that
fateful day when my successor arrived unannounced to see
our church, to visit with the pulpit committee and look at the
parsonage, I felt an awful twinge of uncertainty. I kept
thinking, "What am I doing? Twelve years of my life are in
this place!" But by that time there was no turning back.
Everything was final. We were launched.

I certainly did not feel the least bit like the monk in the
limerick President Woodrow Wilson was fond of quoting (I
almost wish I had):

> There was a young monk of Siberia
> Whose existence grew drearier and drearier
> 'Til he burst from his cell
> With a hell of a yell
> And eloped with the Mother Superior.

After much prayer on the important matter of where to
spend the sabbatical year, we discovered a charming home
some distance from our former parish, in an area where such
rentals were rarely if ever available. From the beginning, our
children were delighted with their new school and many
friends. The phone that had formerly been such a disturber
of the peace rang so infrequently as to be almost conspicuous
by its silence. When it did ring, everyone in the family
rushed to grab the receiver. At times that was embarrassing,
particularly when my wife's mother was calling to see if we
were all right.

We acquired two rabbits and a mother cat who saw fit to

present us regularly with a litter of her impossible-to-give-away kittens. At Christmas time we hiked out into a snowy forest and had the experience of cutting down our first tree that will *not* be best remembered for its symmetrical beauty. After it was decorated we gathered in the reflection of colored lights to sing carols and gaze fondly at our prize acquisition. It was good to bathe in the atmosphere of doing one thing at a time.

The winter of our deep content passed swiftly, and soon we met the arrival of spring out wandering along the winding pathways of a nearby woods. This was all new and wonderful to me. For many years I had not seen what was mine to see. I had been too busy. Life had been so upclose, uptight, upbeat. We discovered the lavish display of God's exquisite handiwork in the wild flowers hidden off the beaten path just waiting to be discovered. I felt the power of William Blake's words:

> To see a World in a grain of sand
> And a Heaven in a Wild Flower,
> Hold Infinity in the palm of your hand,
> And eternity in an hour.

Gratefully I reveled in the enchanting wonder of the good earth, attempting to employ my Second Sight to psych out the spiritual symbolism of everything in sight. For a space of time my whole world was the nearby forest with its bubbling stream that became more and more an enchanting cathedral of nature filled with hidden wonder. In this atmosphere I felt my soul reborn. I shall never forget those unfolding days.

As my sabbatical leave stretched into a second year, one of our denomination's most publicized churches began search-

ing for a senior minister. Being unemployed and having a
few friends in this church, I was more than a little interested
in future developments. Much to my delight an invitation
was dispatched with episcopal approval inviting me to preach
at a worship service and be interviewed by the pulpit committee. I felt both honored and elated. The feeling of rightness hovered over this prospect with pleasurable vibrations.
Subsequently the committee voted unanimously to offer me
the senior ministry of their church. I was thrilled beyond
words. My spirits soared. I knew that unquestionably the
Lord had such a church in mind for me. The whole world
was rolling at my feet. God was my chief benefactor; indeed
he and I were in complete agreement concerning my future.
This was all part of his glorious plan.

There was one hitch, however. This invitation was subject
to the approval of two episcopal leaders and several administrative advisors. Permission was indirectly denied. By indirectly I mean that no one ever said a definite "yes" or "no."
It was just that I had been decided against by an intransigent
authority that seemed set against me. I did receive a letter
from my episcopal leader curtly detailing how in our denomination a local church could not call a minister, that this
was the prerogative of the bishop. Amen! But why had I
received episcopal approval to visit the church in the first
place, let alone be interviewed as a ministerial candidate? My
golden moments in the sun of anticipation had been reduced
to the absurdity of a burst soap bubble, an exploded desire, a
broken dream that I carried in grief down a darkened stair-
way into the depth of my being, hoping somehow to bury its
memory forever, but never quite able to do so.

Later I learned that behind the scenes there had been a
rush of political activity, as several church administrators,

including one who desired the job for himself, met in secret session unbeknown to the bishop in charge, to control the destiny of the church that had requested me to be its pastor. It was decided that no connectional church of that size and strategic importance was going to have as their minister a man whose loyalty to the denomination was in question. Of course, my being on sabbatical and admittedly having independent tendencies only served to confirm their suspicions.

Shock and anger blended into disbelief at this naked display of power politics in the life of the church. I felt the animal need to revenge myself.

Then one day I took my family for a walk in the woods. Totally absorbed in the besetting problem, I inadvertently leaned against a tree and began to meditate. I noted the deep stillness in this object of nature, how the tree limbs seemed to reach up toward the sun, as though celebrating the source of creative energy.

Gradually through focusing, relaxing, seeking the mind of Christ, a measure of Second Sight was supplied. It appeared that this tree was living out a plan of life in trustful companionship. Becoming absolutely still, I felt a strange internal throb and knew as surely as I have ever known anything that Christ within was carrying out the purpose born in my life despite the outward circumstances of a deep desire refused.

Suddenly I was set free by this awareness, as a soothing breeze swept over my face like a peaceful benediction. I recalled a verse in John's Gospel. After the resurrection, Jesus rejoined his disciples and the Scripture says, "He breathed on them." That is precisely what I felt in that moment. In fact, it seemed that I could almost lean back and be a spectator to the events, watching God take my life and use

it as he would see fit. I could identify with the words of the
famous farewell Shakespeare put in the mouth of Cardinal
Wolsey in reply to his servant's question, "How does your
grace?"

> Why, well;
> Never so truly happy, my good Cromwell.
> I know myself now; and I feel within me
> A peace above all earthly dignities,
> A still quiet conscience.[1]

Looking down the path I saw an unforgettable sight. Each
member of my family was leaning against a tree . . . outward eyes closed, inward eyes open.

During the sabbatical leave my wife gave birth to our
fourth child, a beautiful baby boy. In so doing, she contracted
an almost archaic illness known in layman's terms as "delayed
childbirth fever." Several years ago this disease was the
known killer of countless mothers following delivery, but
certainly not today.

For twenty-seven days she was hospitalized, while I acted
out the role of substitute mother for three children and a
baby. During the first few days of her hospital siege, the
doctors were unable to diagnose her sickness, and their puz-
zlement caused me to ponder the complete unreality of this
awful happening. She was actually dying and it seemed that
no one was doing anything to help. I could not have felt more
helpless, standing by and watching the person I love more
than anyone else in the world suffer excruciating pain,
listening to her voice pronounce words of need with increasing difficulty, and hearing the physician state unequivocally
that her condition was critical. At last the proper antibiotic

1. *King Henry the Eighth*, Act III, Sc. 2, ll. 376–80.

was introduced, and she took the first steps on the long road to recovery.

Our home became the scene of a vigil of prayer, and for the first time in their lives my children witnessed their father reduced to tears. At a crisis moment my wife asked me to call a spiritual life center where prayer is offered for people around the clock. I still remember the voice of a calm, deeply spiritual woman whose healing words challenged me with the perspective of her Second Sight: "Your wife really is completely in God's hands. She always has been and always will be." I mumbled some inadequate appreciation, stretched out on the floor, closed my eyes, relaxed—and began to feel the lifting of consciousness and the return of strength overcoming the paralysis of futility so that I could get on with what I had to do.

Somehow I knew that God was present in all that awful misery, helping me in the dark, keeping me on my feet so that those entrusted to my keeping would not be neglected or harmed. Gradually I became aware of the light that had been shining in the dark all the time, even when I had failed to see it.

One afternoon while in reflection I thought of something in R. L. Stevenson's story "Ebb Tide" when he speaks of the lighted stage on which all men stand before God—that no matter how hopeless life appears, "empty beach, empty house, empty sea," we still have all of heaven for our audience. We are never out of God's eternal sight, no matter how dreadful the circumstances. As I look back with Second Sight on those anguish-filled moments of my life, I now see them as contributing to the whole of what God had for me to experience. He was about the work of shaping events beyond my inadequate power to comprehend.

From time to time through that ordeal I recalled a sermon
I had read by Dr. John Gossip which he preached the Sunday
following his wife's sudden death. His sermon topic was
"But When Life Tumbles In, What Then?" "You people in
the sunshine," he said, "may believe in faith; we people in
the shadow must believe it. We have nothing else." I must
confess that through those bleak moments that is all I had—
just the Second Sight glimpse of a flickering candlelight
faith set against the awful midnight dark. But it was sufficient.

There were other experiences that helped, that were
glimmers of light.

"Don, will you take this one?" The funeral director's
voice was unusually solemn and insistent.

"The family doesn't have a minister. Their nineteen-year-
old boy was killed in Viet Nam. He was due to come home
within a month but . . . he got hit. It will be a full-fledged
military funeral. Please will you take it?"

Frankly I had been through sufficient emotional wringers
of late to last me a lifetime, but I could not say no.

The family sat huddled a few feet from a silver-colored
coffin covered with the brightly contrasting stars and stripes.
The rest of the room was filled with an honor guard from
nearby Ft. Knox. I read the Twenty-third Psalm and spoke
briefly. At the graveside, three rounds of rifle fire pierced the
cemetery silence, and from a nearby hill a bugler played
Taps. A committal was read. The flag was precisely folded
and handed to the mother. It was over. Nineteen years stuck
in the ground.

I was sick with anger, frustration, and sorrow for the
family, not to mention the nagging disturbance of an in-

operative Second Sight. I could not seem to penetrate the surface level of this senseless experience. "Lord, what do you want me to see in this?" I prayed inwardly. That prayer of need had a focusing effect. Gradually I began to see what I had almost missed. She could not have been more than fifteen—the sister of the fallen soldier. She was the one person in that crowd of mourners who seemed to drink in every word uttered in the funeral service. I watched her tenderly ministering to her family with tears welling in her eyes. Somehow she seemed to know what to say and what to do. More important, she never faltered, just kept on keeping on. It was beautiful.

Then she turned toward me, and I was astonished by her expression. Rarely have I seen such peace on any face. The grief, the hurt, the loss, the all-out effort to serve her family's needs had softly shaped her facial features to a Christlike expression of love and understanding—and there Christ was, looking at me through her. And to think I had almost missed him!

As we neared the close of the sabbatical leave, our financial situation became predictably critical. My morale was at an all-time low. Adversity was stalking our path once more, and the sheer enormity of its presence was enough to "bend me out of shape," as my teenage daughter so graphically puts it. With speaking engagements trailing off and the cost of living devouring our savings, I began seeking employment of any kind to stave off the wolf at the door. I recall feeling a surge of envy and resentment every time I saw someone use food stamps in a grocery store. We had come a long way from the protection of denominational unionism (guaranteed wages) to the economic straits of testing the elasticity of the dollar.

Jobs were difficult to find, but at last a good friend helped me secure part-time employment as a laborer in a furniture warehouse. This was a genuinely schizoid time in my life. One day I would be unloading a boxcar of sofas, the next evening I would be in a city three hundred miles away preaching to a crowd in a downtown church.

The job proved to be a double blessing. First of all it provided a paycheck to cover our basic necessities; and then it was great therapy. Still there were times when I felt sorry for myself—mostly at night. Almost unconsciously I would repeat a litany of negatives:

"I can't believe this is happening to us.

"Could anything be more absurd.

"We are victims of a corrupt system.

"Why us? Why us? Why us?"

But regurgitating the predicament served no useful purpose. In fact, in a tragically stupid way, I was impressing my subconscious with the futility of the situation and to that end was blinded by close-up circumstances. I wallowed in the mire of the immediate problem.

Friends would stop by our house from time to time. Most of them had been members of our church. Our mutual role-playing on these occasions was in one sense painfully unreal, yet in another wildly funny. These visiting sessions did not seem unlike scenes I have witnessed countless times in funeral homes. Everyone attempts to say the right thing while not asking too many questions that would prove disturbing to the bereaved, and carefully avoiding direct reference to the present circumstances. So much was left unsaid, but I could see it in their eyes—like they were really asking, "How could anyone get so messed up?"

Running helped! I would jog several miles every day,

regardless of weather conditions, and for the first time in my life I actually enjoyed working out. Physical exhaustion of this kind provided a much-needed anesthetic. No escape could have been more pleasant. Sometimes when loping along I would fantasize the composing of a letter to my bishop. It was heroically vindictive, a grand telling-off of the person I considered most responsible for my present trouble. Of course, the hypothetical letter was never put on paper. I suppose at the time my thoughts served a useful purpose, but now I see that my preoccupation with such a negative attitude only wasted time and served to keep me bound in the chains of noncreative resentment.

Then one night during an unusually long run, I experienced an extraordinary flashback of an evening spent several months earlier with the prophetess Jeane Dixon. We met in the home of a friend and, after introductions, were escorted to a private room where Mrs. Dixon clutched my hand and proceeded to project what she considered to be my future over the next several months. She stated categorically that I would be passing through a dark tunnel of experience, but that I should concentrate on the light at the end of the tunnel. Despite her celebrity status and highly publicized gift, I did not take her prediction all that seriously. At the time a dark tunnel seemed an impossible suggestion. Now, running and remembering, I thought of the tunnel and what Mrs. Dixon had said about the light at the end; the thought served as a good focal point for some time to come.

During these days a wonderful little woman with the most appropriate name came into our lives—Mrs. Faith. Not only was she an extremely compassionate person, she was also a resourceful teacher of spiritual truth. For one thing, she spent considerable time teaching us what she called the law of attraction. She lectured at length with her heavy German accent on the need to get a strong mental picture of our heart's desire, making sure that it was of the highest order and within the Father's will. This specific inward seeing, she indicated, would impress our subconscious mind with an exact command. She warned us not to give attention to any negative thoughts that might invade our consciousness and attempt to diminish the picture.

"If you give attention to the negative," she said, "you are undermining your best interest." (Jesus said it well—"Do not judge by appearances," John 7:24.) "If your desire picture is in harmony with the highest and best you know, then you can affirm with all your heart that despite whatever the appearance may be, with God all things are possible."

As I look back on our attempts to put Mrs. Faith's wise teaching into practice, I am still amazed at the speed with which things began to happen. After much discussion, we visualized our ministry in a church situation where we would be free to serve as we were led by the Spirit. We knew beyond any shadow of doubt that we really needed to be involved in a local church situation, but the church would necessarily need to be totally autonomous. Shortly thereafter three opportunities were presented to us, each of which was almost a perfect replica of the prototype we had visualized. We decided to accept the church that took us geographically to the far Northwest. Six very happy people journeyed hundreds of miles across plains, hills, rivers, and mountains, and much further in spiritual significance, to find our hearts' desire.

At last the sabbatical had come to an end. As I look back, I can honestly say that the difficulties we encountered along the way were never the result of our not having enough belief in God, nor did they result from failure to take a leap of faith. I do not believe we could be found wanting in this regard. It was just that we had not developed sufficient knowing concerning God's truth within. We had not learned to see through the veiled processes of ebb and flow with the deeper wisdom Wordsworth once described as a "passionate intuition." This is the knowing that can set one free.

# ✳ 4

## WHEN
## GOD WANTS A CITY

"I am sick of provincial churches that show no interest in the needs of their society. Occasionally, just occasionally, when I see a Christian or group of Christians take a stand on a moral issue against great odds, I want to shout, 'That's really it! That's Christianity.' But it happens so rarely. . . ."

—A housewife and mother, aged 31.

# WHEN
# GOD WANTS A CITY

My friend Jerry had been minister of a strong village church for seventeen years. Although it was located only a few miles from a large, sprawling city, the church was in a next-door county area classified as semi-rural. Through these years he witnessed the transformation of his parish from a sleepy country community to a mushrooming land-boom area—at length to degenerate into a blighted rural ghetto. Inaccessible terrain, uncreative political provincialism, and lack of legal control to safeguard the use of the land had checked the county's growth and development. However, there was no conceivable direction the nearby overcrowded city could move except toward this county that was virtually unsuited for such expansion.

The deplorable conditions of the county included: public schools in half-day sessions; teachers leaving in search of higher wages; a history of continuous school bond and levy defeats; potentially capable community leaders moving away; a host of vacant houses; inadequate police protection; exorbitant utility rates; an unworkable township government structure; no agencies for family counseling; no health care

or youth activities; no public parks; no YMCA or YWCA; no
research, planning staff, or citizen's group in the county to
deal with existing conditions. In short it was a very bad
scene.

In 1965, Jerry's church undertook an intensive self-study
investigation of their role in the community and how they
could best serve the needs of the people there. This precari-
ous undertaking in itself was a radical departure from the
uncritical attitude of most churches toward their community
relationships. After many soul-searching sessions, the self-
study committee of one hundred proposed to the congregation an incredible motion—that their church property be
deeded over to the community as an ecumenical service
center. It would provide a planned parenthood clinic, day-
care facilities for children of working women, a youth center,
a lay academy for theological training, an institute for counseling, a home for the elderly, and a hospital for the sick. Of
course, the plan was fantastically ambitious, but there was
no denying one hundred challenging voices crying in their
local wilderness that something unprecedented be done.

Their dream was for a total ministry where "no need
would be too small, no problem too great, no concern out of
their area, and no one turned away." In the face of overwhelming need, a conviction grew among the committee for
a detailed community plan directed toward a complete program for future county development, and all undergirded by
a sense of Christian stewardship. As they saw it, the first
order of business was the sacrifice of their church facility in
order to get the project off the ground. The committee report
was submitted to the church's official board with no small
amount of fear and trembling. To everyone's amazement,

the entire package was unanimously approved with very little hassle.

News of this happening was picked up quickly on the denominational grapevine, and at first hearing several administrative leaders of the church hierarchy enthusiastically applauded the creative approach that had been set forth. But when the bishop of the area learned that one of his half-million-dollar church properties might be sacrificed, notwithstanding the cause, he vetoed the project and called the "brash" young minister on the carpet.

Jerry showed me the penciled notes of that unforgettable interview. The bishop informed him that he had the ability to be one of the outstanding leaders of the denomination's conference, that he was intelligent and very persuasive, but that he had a blind spot. He could only see one community and had become so active in this community's affairs that he was neglecting "the spiritual." "Your people are wanting to be fed more 'spiritually.'"

As I read these notes, I could not help wondering how a congregation could be persuaded to allow their beloved place of worship to be given over as a community center unless the pastor had been feeding them something approximating spiritual food.

The bishop further indicated that there were more important communities than this one, and that Jerry should join the denominational team, accept a promotion, and not waste his valuable ministerial training on such a hopeless parish. He was accused of being against the denominational church, and told that this proposal (to sell the church property) was an example of his conspiring to get out from under the mother church authority. The bishop stated emphatically that he would not buy this idea, and that it was the consensus of Jerry's friends that he had great ability but he was not "spiritual" enough.

Following his episcopal dressing down, Jerry was amazed to discover that many of his ministerial colleagues were behaving rather strangely toward him. For instance, one denominational administrator took Jerry into his hotel room after glancing up and down the hallway like a bad actor in a grade B mystery movie, closed the door, locked it, and whispered confidentially, "Although I agree with what you and your church have proposed to do, I will not be able to be seen with you again in public." What he did not say, but what was self-evident, was that the cost of associating with a denominational outcast might mean risking advancement when the bishop made out his yearly list of church appointments.

I read a number of letters from well-placed ministerial friends who praised Jerry's project enthusiastically but who never spoke a public word in his defense. Jerry was now impaled on a lonely cross but was determined to see this project through, no matter what the cost. Having set himself over against the power structure of his denomination, he had to suffer the agonizing penalty of losing the ministry of his local church. But there was no other way. The totality of his inward pain only intensified the conviction that his cause was just. At any rate several people standing at a safe distance kept telling him this was so.

It was the biblical word that held him to his course during that dark and trying night of his soul. Day by day, through reading, focusing, and meditating, he attempted to get some Second Sight on his situation. One morning while reading the thirty-second chapter of Jeremiah, several words struck fire in his heart. Suddenly he "saw" the spiritual leading beneath the surface level of the Scripture word: " '. . . in accordance with the word of the Lord, . . . "Buy my field . . . , for the right of possession and redemption is yours; buy it for yourself." Then I knew that this was the word of the Lord' " (Jer. 32:8). He believed beyond any shadow of doubt that these words were addressed to him. God did have an ultimate plan and purpose for his life! A deep peace came over him—the first in a long, long time.

Acting on this Second Sight guidance, Jerry searched until he discovered a beautiful piece of farm property. When he attempted to buy it, the owner, figuring he had a sucker on the line, asked an unheard of $85,000 for 110 acres. The property at that time was not worth half that much. Jerry might have laughed in his face. Instead he made out a check for $50 and promised to have the balance in thirty days. Once he confided that his wife was not as much concerned about raising $85,000 as that she wasn't sure they had $50 in their checking account.

Later he invited an architect-engineer friend to look at the property and give his candid opinion of its real worth. This man declared the land to be the most beautiful piece of industrial property he had ever seen. Jerry asked if he would be willing to invest his own money in the property. The architect-engineer agreed and volunteered to invite some of his friends to do the same. Within seven days they had raised over $100,000. Through continued meditation, a Second Sight vision began breaking on the horizon of Jerry's mind.

In his closing sermon at the church from which he was now dismissed, he solemnly asked his people to join him in building something more ambitious than the originally proposed all-purpose community center. He challenged them to join in a true partnership of faith and stewardship by pooling their financial resources, buying land, and building their own model city designed to meet the highest living standards available, and to dedicate it all as a living project to the glory of God. Speaking of this city as a place where men could live "creatively, productively and healthfully," he dramatically set three test questions before the congregation: "Does God want this action taken? Does he want it done now? Does he want us to do it?"

Those who attended church that morning can still recite almost verbatim the stirring words of Jerry's sermon. The response was overwhelming. People cashed in their life savings, homes were mortgaged, piggy banks were cracked open, money poured in from across the community regardless of religious affiliation, as people young and old heard the clarion call to action. A corporation was formed to sell stock, and sale-value per share increased 400 percent in the first hundred days. This was a fantastic display of group faith ignited by a hope in the future. Even the old-timers begrudgingly admitted the "upstarts" were making things happen that had never happened before. However, the money managers of the area were slow to see the virtue in the project. They had to be convinced.

Jerry plowed ahead, buying land, making his own business contacts, and creating confidence by his sound planning. It took two years of promotive blood, sweat, and tears until by the grace of God a transformation in attitude took place, and the millionaires, captains of industry, and presidents of companies, sensing the potential in this project, began clamoring to get aboard the bandwagon by making investments and buying property for their enterprises in the new city. In a moment of reflection, Jerry once told me of the many times during those first two struggling years when, if he had been five minutes too early or five minutes too late, a crucial transaction for the life of the project would not have taken place.

"The only plausible explanation for this good fortune," as he explained, "is that we have been led by God all the way. After all, this is his city and his will shall be done."

The corporation is still busily engaged in buying open land on which later additions to the new city will be constructed. One day in Jerry's office I saw an architect's plan for the new city. It is an immensely creative projection that includes high density townhouse apartments beautifully situated in an open setting and "green belts" of meadowland for play areas and parks, as opposed to the one house–one lot sprawl that characterizes the topsy-turvy swell of suburbia in most American cities. Even the shopping areas are designed for accessibility and include a model transportation system, guaranteeing rapid access to and from various places in the city. This plan was so conceived that not a single human value would be compromised. Asking what seemed a legitimate question, I inquired if only the wealthy could afford the tremendous living advantages of the new city. I was quickly informed that it will be a place for anyone who wishes to live there regardless of racial origin, national background, religious affiliation, or economic status. The plans are all-inclusive in provision for open housing, employment, education, recreation, shipping, cultural development.

Sometime ago the governor of the state formally opened a new industrial air strip which now operates adjacent to the city area. Hangars are being constructed that will also provide office space in the same buildings. This one innovation alone will allow for considerable time-saving in the average workday—another attractive inducement to a potential investor.

One of the vice-presidents of Jerry's corporation, bubbling with enthusiasm for the spectacular progress of the project, asked me rhetorically, "How do you think we propose to heat and air-condition the new city?" I had not the faintest idea other than the traditional methods. Smiling expansively he volunteered, "We will do it with the trash that the city is trying to find some place to dump." Unquestionably one of the problems that plagues all modern cities is disposing of its waste. The "New City" planning department has an answer. Using a novel technological method, the city area will be heated and air-conditioned by transforming the waste material into serviceable energy.

Today, nearly four thousand acres have been purchased, and over seven hundred shares of stock have been sold. More financial help is on the way as the city begins to take shape and a glorious dream is being fulfilled.

I asked Jerry, now president of the prosperous new city land development corporation, if he ever experienced a twinge of bitterness concerning his broken relationship with the church. His answer was not surprising.

"I feel I was called by God to the ministry. I was ordained by the will of God to serve his church. My right of having a church was stolen from me in the same way that thieves would break in and rob a bank, but I have found something else along the way that has changed everything. I have seen a vision and I still have a ministry. If the bishop and the denomination are correct in their denunciation of me and the work to which I am committed, they will be blessed. But if we are right, we will be blessed."

Viewing the town springing up through the Second Sight

vision of a revolutionary spirit—socially, religiously, eco-
nomically, racially, and culturally dedicated to the principle
of helping conserve the best for all the people and making
responsible use of the land—it is not difficult to see who is
receiving a harvest of blessing.

Jerry referred me to the words of Jeremiah, and read aloud
from this chapter of Scripture as movingly as ever I have
heard anything read. But then he had lived the words of the
ancient book, and that gave his voice the ring of authority
and authenticity.

" 'For thus says the Lord: Just as I have brought all this
great evil upon this people, so I will bring upon them all the
good that I promise them. Fields shall be bought in this land
of which you are saying, It is a desolation. . . . Fields shall
be bought for money, and deeds shall be signed and sealed
and witnessed . . . ; for I will restore their fortunes, says
the Lord' " (Jer. 32:42–44).

As he finished reading, a burst of sunlight broke through
the dark clouds of a dreary day and fell upon his face. I was
transfixed for a moment, considering what a beautiful spirit
this man is. In that instant I recognized the necessity for the
verse in the Book of Ecclesiasticus: "Let us now praise famous men." Second Sight revealed the strength of Jerry's
life—a God-given strength equal to the task of bringing a
magnificent vision to concrete reality with the help of God.
No question about it; he is winning the battle. But if you
look closely, the wounds of combat are still visible and the
tears are occasionally present. But the healing Spirit of Christ
is at work, too, tending to the hurt places, wiping away the
tears, and fulfilling the purpose of this man's life. I simply
thanked God for eyes to see.

The pattern revealed in Jerry's life—seeking with Second Sight for inward guidance, gaining a perspective on God's grandest plan, then going out to put this plan into action—appears utterly Christlike because it is so sanely balanced. Such an example fires a twofold challenge at the modern Christian. Of course we are called to serve God in the world, but we are likewise called to seek his guidance in the cathedral of our souls. Openness to the world without a corresponding openness to spiritual replenishing produces the sort of Christian response that is well meaning but tragically lacking in directional power.

Teilhard de Chardin suggested that we should venture inward for spiritual equipping so that we can venture outward prepared to serve the mission God has for us in the world. He called this two-way street the "double thread" of life—going in for the sake of going out.

This is not a matter of either-or. I believe a person is so constituted that he needs the spiritual refreshment of time alone with God. But he also needs the creative outlet of service to others in order to serve the external purpose of his life. I have yet to meet a person who did not need the heightened consciousness experience of an Upper Room where he can retreat from the lower dimensional encounters of the street. The street is so much with us. Its din is in our ears, its dust in our clothes, its smell in our nostrils, its transitory sights before our eyes—its negative spirit seeps into our very being. We need to climb the ladder of meditation and find our way into a time alone with our indwelling Christ under the canopy of God's sovereign plan. But we must not stay there removed from the street scene, no matter how uplifting the experience. We must return to the street, for our ministries are there, and most of all, through the refocusing of Second Sight, we see that God is there too. I repeat, this is not a matter of either-or, it is both-and. If this were not so, Jerry would not have seen the vision of the new city, and for lack of faith-action the vision would not have become a reality.

In the places where I have traveled, the expressions of confusion on this matter have troubled me deeply. Repeatedly I have heard the most well-meaning people state emphatically: "You have to make up your mind which you will be—an activist or a pray-er, a servant or a mystic, a do-gooder or a hermit. You must make up your mind." This is such a phony set of choices. It is a product of the modern churchman's desperate desire to establish himself somewhere in these changing times by hugging to his mind a maximum security concept—which is in reality a half-truth. I have come away from these "either-or" people recognizing how incomplete they are—and how little they see. I am now utterly enlisted in the cause of helping fragmented Christians develop Second Sight sufficient to see their lives against the perfect wholeness of Christ—or at least freeing their willingness to consider the possibility that something is lacking in their lives, and that is a perspective of their God-given potentiality to be a more balanced person. To this end I frequently do nothing more than tell them Jerry's story.

I cannot escape the feeling that we have been living through an inbetween time that might best be described as a "hinge of history." Perhaps this "hinge time" is like that which the Russian writer, Anton Chekhov, pictured in his play, *The Cherry Orchard*. The play symbolized the transformation from the old Russian imperialism to the new day of The Revolution. In that twilight zone of transition a family of the aristocracy is forced to sell their country home and orchard to an emerging serf. Then comes the fateful day.

Inside the house the departing family sobs tears of regret for their great loss, while outside a new family impatiently waits to enter. But the curtain does not fall there to close out the story neatly. The stage is left empty. The sounds of doors being closed and carriages driving off are heard. Then everything is quiet and from far off in the orchard comes the sound of an ax striking a tree.

I believe such a moment in history has happened to us. A new family is moving in. Change is inevitable. The old house will never be the same. The new age is here. Certainly the Christian enterprise can ill afford to remain frozen in some inadequate faith response, holding up tattered toy dreams of the past. If Christianity is to supply the answers that are needed for today's problems, we must recognize that Christ calls us both to the experience of spiritual empowering in order to develop our Second Sight and to the valley of human need, to minister on the street level where we live, that the inward may be translated to the outward.

The thrust of the Christian life is not the Upper Room set over against the street level. Rather it is the total embodiment of spiritual awareness or Second Sight in responsible Christ-centered action so plainly evident in the life of my friend Jerry.

# 5

# A NEW CHURCH
# FOR THE NEW AGE

"Don't get me wrong. I don't hate the church. I just want it to be better than it is. I want it to be alive—not what some old deacon thinks is alive but my kind of alive. . . ."
—The 20-year-old daughter of a deacon.

# A NEW CHURCH
# FOR THE NEW AGE

A group of college-age people from a variety of religious backgrounds had been meditating. The majority were stretched out on my office floor. The room was filled with lively vibrations. After leading them through the exercises for relaxing, focusing, and centering on the screen of the mind, I asked for their Second Sight perspective on the contemporary church.

During the next several minutes of eager response, I did not hear the usual putting down of the religious establishment, or the customary scorn of church hypocrisy. There was just concern, at times so heartfelt one could have wished for several million church people to hear. They spoke mostly of narrow denominationalism and dead worship in dead churches. I was pleasantly surprised that no one felt the need to demonstrate a grievance by taking over our church sanctuary during Sunday morning worship with floating balloons, interpretive dancing, guitar music, folk hymns, costumes, or a parade of banners. No one insisted that we "get back to Psalm 150." Rather there was just the impassioned request for increased emphasis on spiritual development for all ages and the unanimous feeling of need for an open, adventurous church life that would give priority to this sort of experience. This church, each one declared with urgent enthusiasm, must come into being, and now!

One boy kept insisting that the contemporary church is exactly like the famous painting of George Washington crossing the Delaware during the Revolutionary War. He recalled that his sixth grade history teacher had pointed to a large size reprint of the original and had declared emphatically that this was undoubtedly the way it was on that memorable occasion when Washington led his men across the Delaware River to attack the British at Philadelphia.

Later the boy learned that while such an event did take place, the time-honored painting we have of it is full of distortion and inaccuracy. In the first place, the boat in which Washington is seen is not the sort of craft that was used for river crossings of a military nature. Such a boat would have been long and canoe-shaped. Meteorological records reveal that on this particular night the weather was not clear as the picture indicates, but snowy, and the visibility was extremely poor. Furthermore, according to historical reference, there were no ice floes in the river as illustrated. The soldiers in the boat are seen holding their muskets with the barrels pointed up. Any soldier worth his salt would protect his musket from moisture by keeping the barrel pointed down. The stars and stripes flag observed in the painting could not have been used because it was not as yet authorized by Congress. And finally, George Washington would not have been foolish enough to stand in so small a boat. He was reputed to be a brave man but not a stupid one. Evidently the artist who did the painting not only was nowhere near the scene he so vividly portrayed—he hadn't even researched his project.

The young speaker went on to say, "The picture we have of the Christian church today as a continuation of the fellowship Jesus set in motion is a gross distortion. The early church described in the Book of Acts was a body of people filled with spiritual power and destined by the purpose of God to express his will. By no stretch of the imagination is this what we have today." Though his conclusions may have suffered a bit from overstatement, we did at least agree with the general thrust of his argument.

Later that evening in a time of personal Second Sight reflection I meditated on what sort of church would emerge in the new age. In an overview scan I saw a host of people hypnotized by the tragic notion that in order to be a Christian you must decide on a single theological or institutional view of Christ and be stuck with it forever. I saw these people walking through a valley enjoying the sight of a beautiful lake. After hiking farther on the trail a magnificent mountain comes into view. Now because of a bend in the path they are unable to see the lake and the mountain at the same time. They must make a selection as to which one will hold their attention. It seems a terrible choice, for both are beautiful. However there is an alternative. If they really desire to see the lake and the mountain at the same time, they must climb higher.

It is always risky business, however, to climb higher. Gaining a Second Sight perspective can be a profoundly disturbing experience. The person seeking higher awareness is in danger of discovering truth that could precipitate a crisis in his life when outmoded elements of faith on a variety of levels must be discarded so that relevant ones may be learned.

A few years ago my wife and a friend dragged me off to

hear a woman speak on spiritual healing in the life of the church. The mere mention of the subject sent me into flights of unreasonable denunciation. A seminary professor had told me that God simply does not heal anyone today, except through the practice of medical science, and anyone who thinks otherwise is a "weirdo." I accepted his point of view with the naïve assurance that surely this man with all his academic degrees must know what he was talking about. At length I had succeeded in developing a blind prejudice because I had never taken the trouble to examine the claims of spiritual healing.

On this occasion I was all prepared to give the "weirdo" healer a real hatchet job by asking a series of questions designed to embarrass her. Much to my amazement the speaker turned out to be a marvelously intelligent, articulate, sophisticated woman, who presented the case for healing in the life of the church in a persuasively winsome fashion. She mentioned little, if anything, about healing per se, but spoke mostly about the love of God, about which I could not argue. Listening to her was like hearing the crystal clear ringing of a bell after being in silence, or being overtaken by blinding light while in darkness. Over the next few days I experienced a genuine faith crisis in struggling to climb higher over the obstacles of a preconceived notion, intellectual pride, and an inadequate understanding of the subject.

Finally my mind opened long enough to try an experiment. Along with several others I began praying for the wholeness of certain people, utilizing the techniques this woman had suggested. We soon discovered that while we could not help everyone, we could help some. And the "some" who were helped stated in no uncertain terms that they were lifted to receive the healing touch through the expression of God's love in those who prayed. Their testimonies were pretty convincing, so the healing ministry continued. Today I believe that praying for the wholeness of persons has a legitimate place in the ministry of any church, for it fits so perfectly within the framework of a serving fellowship—which is the larger Second Sight view of the church. The New Testament writer James underscores this: "Is any among you sick? Let him call for the elders of the church, and let them pray over him . . ." (James 5:14).

As my visualization continued, I returned to the time of my sabbatical journeys when I saw the contemporary church at close range. Speaking in far-away places and meeting new people had been exciting and fascinating work for several weeks—even though two planes on which I was riding almost crashed. However, the more I had visited persons in all kinds of churches, conferences, retreats, and a host of other places, the more I came to realize on a large scale what I had always known in a limited sense. That is, that large numbers of church people seem to have an involuntary old age reflex; they have closed minds toward new ideas that threaten their static condition.

This is not to say that my hosts along the way were anything but polite, friendly, and generally enthusiastic concerning the approaches I suggested. But at times it seemed I was somehow involved in Eugene O'Neill's play *Strange Interlude,* in which the schizoid-like actors are saying one set of lines to each other and quite another to themselves. The church leaders might say to me, "That is a great idea; maybe we ought to try it." But to themselves it would be, "This approach is too far out for us; it would never work here."

I felt an increasing frustration over the lack of openness

in the contemporary church, or at least what I saw of it. It would be unfair to infer that the people I visited did not give my viewpoints a gracious hearing. It was just that, in general, they seemed unwilling to synthesize into a personal faith response something coming from outside their traditional approach.

Recently I heard about several members of a strong denominational church who ganged up on their "let's keep everything cool" pastor for the purpose of inviting a well-known spiritual life leader to address their congregation. The minister passed off the unpleasant duty to his youthful assistant (known for his prejudice against developing the spiritual life), who wrote the leader a terse, indifferent letter of invitation and instruction, stating unequivocally that the proposed Sunday evening service would last no longer than one hour. The leader would be limited to exactly thirty minutes and if his wife, a talented speaker in her own right, was to participate, this would have to come out of his time. Incidentally, the letter failed to give directions on how to reach the church, and no arrangements were made for overnight lodging. The outworkings of a closed mind are interesting to behold.

As I looked back over my travels, I remembered visiting churches deeply dedicated to creating "a secular congregation on mission to the world"—an arresting slogan. The social passion of these people is directed toward "restructuring the broken framework of our society" and becoming "fully responsible" in the area of secular concern. They kept repeating that "the Ultimate [which is the symbol they use when speaking of Christ or God] is only found in the world and is to be celebrated there"—another slogan. It is amazing how slogan-conscious these activist people are. It is an exceedingly ambitious goal they have set for themselves, particularly without much help from the "Ultimate," whom many of them consider to be largely a mythological authority symbol. However, they are energetic. They are swinging with a swinging age, using all the right slogans and handling a dozen things at once.

I recalled visiting in churches that have plunged into what they refer to as spiritual renewal through the formation of prayer-study groups with an emphasis on the disciplined life—an extraordinary adventure in these days. I have witnessed the nighttime gathering of young suburban couples who have left the supper dishes undone, and their children in the care of baby sitters, to attend a prayer group meeting for the purpose of getting "filled up." Unfortunately many of these "filled up" ones have not seriously considered the other side of the coin—the "emptying out" in service to a neighbor in deepest need. But they are at least aware that the Gospel according to St. Mark is located in the Bible and that it is within the capacity of man to sit quietly in a prayer circle for up to five minutes without saying a word. This is no small accomplishment.

There were churches along the way of my travels whose ministers seemed passionately engrossed in defending the "old morality" against the so-called "new morality." They attacked with unchained fury the idea of voluntary ethics based on St. Augustine's injunction to "love God and do what you like." In this category I have noted much emphasis on "knowing the Bible." But it is often a matter of memorizing Scripture proof texts to beef up ethical viewpoints and to overwhelm the opposition with a quote on every conceivable subject. No one could rightly accuse these people of being biblically illiterate—a bit haughty but not illiterate.

I recalled preaching in churches of various theological persuasions and temperaments, some of whom were typical white middle-class groups, faithfully implementing their denominational program with unquestioning fidelity, like innocent sheep following whoever is up front playing shepherd. Lay and ministerial leadership in so many of these churches was heartbreakingly unimaginative and apathetic. I have heard church people with tears in their eyes crying out for creative preaching that teaches people how to live in accordance with spiritual laws, for a church program designed to produce saints instead of disinterested, turned-off organization members.

Teilhard de Chardin once spoke of "the immobilists" as those who sit by the fire telling the same old stories while the rest of mankind has simply walked away sadly. I had witnessed this scene repeatedly in major churches across the country. It is "the rest of mankind" with whom I am most concerned. These are the ones who no longer see because they have seen too much of one room in one house of faith, and whose ears have grown dull from listening too long to sanctimonious voices chanting a one-way approach in a dead-end corridor of belief. These are the victims of a closed-minded provincialism, a lack of authentic openness, and a limited religious perspective that obscures the Christ who is Lord of all life, full-orbed in personality, all-embracing in love, and multi-splendored in meaning.

The store was crowded and I was waiting for a clerk to fill my order. All at once I was confronted by a hawkish-looking little man who had selected me out of all the people in the store to hear the outpouring of his religious views. He began speaking in a high squeaky voice—words popped out of his mouth like a repeating rifle.

"You think things are bad right now." (At that moment our city was in the grips of a paralyzing bus strike.) "Just wait . . . God is going to turn the moon blood red. He's going to shake the foundations of the earth. Then in a roll of mighty thunder [he clapped his hands for emphasis] he is going to smash this evil world to pieces. There is only one church where you can be saved from the holocaust that is about to erupt." He gave me the name of a church and its address. "Everyone else is going to hell."

Then he smiled, obviously proud of his daring witness, handed me a piece of 666 literature concerning the mark of the beast, the Antichrist, and the second coming of Christ. He waved his hat to all in the store and departed.

Several college students standing about were breaking up in laughter after observing this outrageous demonstration. I kept thinking, *what a ridiculous distortion!* Then it suddenly dawned on me that while the little man's performance was pretty bizarre, he was guilty of nothing more than egocentric thinking, the "our way is the only way" church pride which is only slightly less irrational than some of the blind loyalties many people have toward the more orthodox denominations.

Then there was that nightmare episode in an ecumenical (if you can believe it) service where a big-shot churchman was expounding on how privileged he was, to have been born and raised as a member of a particular denomination. He went on for nearly an hour bragging about his church's history, theology, outreach. Finally he concluded, "We're the best, we're number one." I'm afraid this man was suffering from something akin to what the undersea explorer Jacques Cousteau calls "the rapture of the depths." Simply put, it is an illusionary sense of self-sufficiency. I kept wondering how the big shot's bravado sounded to the other people in that auditorium who were not of his particular persuasion and how many would simply walk away to God knows where.

There is a fantastic need to open wide the Second Sight eyes of inquiry to see the many paths that lead to Christ's way and to realize how these can actually be blended in a personal faith response. All that is required is an open, adventurous spirit that is willing to come up higher and gain a Second Sight perspective as grand as the mind of Christ.

In my reflection I saw the Christian activist sitting at the feet of the Christian mystic learning the more passive ways of doing the will of God through the disciplines of meditation and contemplation. Then the scene was reversed, as the mystic allowed the activist to teach him how to employ his spiritual development in self-giving service to meet the needs of God's people. I saw the Bible proof-texter becoming an appreciative student of secularist views, thereby gaining a measure of understanding from those who celebrate the world as it is. I visualized the Bible demythologizer learning from the Bible-believing student how to read the Scripture with the heart instead of as a mere cerebral exercise. I saw the organization man of the brand-name denomination listening and looking outside his structural strait jacket and finding creative ways of following Christ, who most assuredly is not the resident patron of any one group that bears his name.

Then it occurred to me if a person could pull together the best in a multitude of faith responses and synthesize these into his life experiences, how much more exciting and joyous the Christian life could be. It seems our problem has always been, as J. B. Phillips put it so aptly, "Our God is too small."

I visualized a local church blending many different forms: a Quaker silent meeting; a Baptist-style baptism by total immersion; an Episcopal form of liturgical worship; the Roman Catholic confessional; a twenty-four-hour open church door for prayer and meditation; the metaphysical churches' approach to the importance of learning how to live in accordance with the spiritual laws; Methodism's recognition of the need for a heart-warming experience; the free churches' call to democracy in action for a local congregation; and the several denominations whose creeds have now been set in modern language for contemporary man; all this in a heightened oneness of expression.

My meditation again took the form of reverie as I relived a worship experience that blended the best from many traditions. One Sunday morning my family and I were ushered to our places in a downtown church. After a period of silence, the choir began the processional singing "Onward Christian Soldiers." Suddenly the organist began playing with thrilling improvisation, trumpets sounded, and a drum began rolling out the cadence as the choir marched down the aisle. The choir sang with enormous joy and occasionally slipped into a higher register with magnificent artistry. The sight of flags moving by and the colorful pageantry made for a deeply moving experience. The sermon was beautifully prepared and delivered, full of positive spiritual meaning for each worshiper as it lifted our personal consciousnesses. There was much time given to guided prayer and meditation, directing people to receive the power from within so that they could be channels to others whose spirit expectancy has diminished. The service closed with the recessional accompanied by the roll of drums and the sound of trumpets.

My oldest daughter whispered, "Daddy, this is the way

it's supposed to be, isn't it? *I feel like something is really happening!*" And something was happening. We were engaged in a mountaintop spiritual experience. Our second eyes were open to see what had been given us to see.

The stream of meditation concerning a new church concept for the new age widened to an expression more vivid than I had previously discerned. At first I saw what appeared to be a church. Maybe it wasn't a church, but it was given the name Christ Center. It was a permanent place where the central emphasis was on helping people of all ages, races, denominations, and nationalities discover the personal presence of the living Christ and the reality of the spiritual life. It offered a multi-dimensional program to challenge the total person on every level of his potential receptivity. It did not seem attached to any denominational organization, but then I couldn't be sure.

The center offered a spiritually alive preaching-teaching emphasis: the application of the spiritual laws found in the Scriptures; training in Second Sight techniques; healing services; daily prayer (meditation-contemplation) services; creative art; creative writing; music and dance programs; sacred concerts; dramatic presentations; athletic camps with adequate facilities; a bookstore and library. In other words, it offered a total consciousness-lifting program.

Christ Center was a place set apart, but it seemed easily accessible to the city and was a place of incomparable natural beauty. It had a Festival Hall constructed of simple rustic materials. The building had a monastic look to it and appeared to house a reception hall, a large dining hall, a kitchen, conference rooms, guest rooms, arts and crafts rooms, office, library, bookstore, and sound studio. A long porch and heavy wooden entrance door lent an attractive appearance to the structure.

The dining room was a great hall with an open beam ceiling and a large fireplace along one wall. Heavy wooden tables and chairs could seat many people. There was a platform at one end of the room for special indoor programs. Around the dining room local artists displayed their works. The food, which was served cafeteria style, was mostly homegrown. Most of the meat, vegetables, milk, eggs, and fruit were raised at Christ Center.

Smaller rooms in the Festival Hall were used for teaching purposes, for small group fellowship, prayer and healing sessions, and special educational activities for children and adults. The rooms were painted in different colors for therapy use. The sound studio was used for making tapes for distribution as people requested them.

I saw an auditorium filled with people experiencing sacred music and dance productions. There were dramatic presentations and consciousness-lifting preaching and teaching. I got the distinct impression that people might come to the center for a weekend, for Sunday, or to spend a week or two for special study or therapy. But always the emphasis was on heightening Christ-consciousness, so that when a person returned to his home environment he did so renewed, refreshed, replenished.

Another facet of the project was the athletic program. Beautifully lighted basketball courts, football field, tennis courts, baseball diamond, and olympic swimming pool had been constructed along with adequate locker facilities. All of the athletic endeavors came under the leadership of spiritually alive people. Many teenagers from across the country were coming to Christ Center for summer camp activity. In addition there were trails and scenic views where people could go to be alone and simply be at one with the Source of all.

As the picture faded, I thought of the college group (incidentally biracial) I had been with that afternoon. The students had spoken of their need for spiritual development, and how so few of their hometown churches had attempted to meet this basic need. Repeatedly they indicated that the leadership of their local churches (both lay and clergy) seemed almost totally preoccupied with contemporary social concerns, to the exclusion of how one grows spiritually. No one questioned the importance of being concerned with social issues, but according to the students the church should give priority attention to developing spiritual awareness. I could scarcely believe what I was hearing. I had long since concluded that one of the primary reasons young people reject the church is its failure to champion certain social causes. This has led to an almost compulsive emphasis on the part of many churches to become as relevant as possible to the secular scene.

Glancing around the room I had noted that each person speaking about the essential need for spiritual attainment was also deeply involved in social action—marching in the protest demonstrations, mobilizing action groups on campus, and giving generous amounts of time to causes that would lift any brother in need. They would agree in a contemporary sense with what Disraeli wrote concerning the youth of England in 1845: "We live in an age when to be young and indifferent can no longer be synonymous." Yet these same people were speaking of the church's need to address itself first and foremost to union with God. Somehow they were perceiving that the realization of God's overall purpose for their lives, activated by an awareness of the Christ's personal presence within, is the key to every situation and need they would experience.

When Jesus said that he must be about "his Father's business," he was saying what the young people have echoed. Self-revelation comes first. When one discovers through Second Sight his true identity in relationship to God, he can then move out to affirm life, to involve himself masterfully because he has an Eternal Master, to bring light in situations of darkness because light now shines through him. But first things must come first; the initial business is developing a spiritual awareness, and from this perspective all else follows.

I could scarcely wait until our next afternoon meeting to get the group's response to the idea of Christ Center. As I related the details of my Second Sight experience, each person in the room began to smile with a look of recognition, as though I was talking about something he had already considered. I had no corner on this glimpse into the future. This was something they too had pictured—perhaps not all at once, but piece by piece over a period of time. The students seemed to feel the importance of establishing a chain of these spiritual life centers across the nation, offering people a place to grow toward the oneness of experience in the Spirit. And if in this country, why not also in the world?

We discussed the conceivability of denominations setting up their own centers for spiritual enrichment, or a local church discovering ways to blend the Christ Center perspective into its own parish life. Then there is the possibility, perhaps more feasible, of an independent approach. There are many possibilities, but at this crucial hour I believe we are under holy orders to respond to what has become the most urgent need perhaps in the history of man—the heightening of consciousness.

With the traditional Christian enterprise, generally speaking, in full-scale retreat along the battle fronts of the world's mind, perhaps the day has finally dawned when people of Christ's Way will reinforce their faith response by blending the best that he has offered through the many ways. Maybe we are now ready to learn the meaning of God's uniting power that leads people from the closed-minded stagnation of closeted opinions to discovering the vast continent of hidden truth through the employment of Second Sight. I believe this is the time of which Christopher Fry wrote:

> Dark and cold we may be, but this
> Is no winter now. The frozen misery
> Of centuries breaks, cracks, begins to move,
> The thunder is the thunder of the floes,
> The thaw, the flood, the upstart Spring.
> Thank God our time is now when wrong
> Comes up to face us everywhere,
> Never to leave us till we take
> The longest stride of soul men ever took.
> Affairs are now soul size
> The enterprise
> Is exploration into God.[1]

1. Christopher Fry, *A Sleep of Prisoners* (New York: Oxford University Press, 1951).

# ▩6

## CELEBRATING
## THE SEASONS OF LIFE

"How is it, that our standing in front of a man wearing a black robe, reading from a black book —watched by a bunch of big-eyed spectators— can cause us to be married?"

—Two young people very much in love.

# ✳ 6

## CELEBRATING
## THE SEASONS OF LIFE

Nancy and Jack have been a part of a college Second Sight group for several months. Both are excellent artists, extremely sensitive, genuinely real people, and very much in love—not the superficial "romance is groovy" type, but love visible in the manner of their sharing and the mutuality of respect one for the other.

One evening they announced matter-of-factly to the group that they planned to be married. It was said so quickly, with so little show of emotion, that I stared at them dumbfounded. They asked me what was wrong and I blurted out, "But who will officiate at your wedding? And where will the wedding be held?"

"Oh, you will," they replied, "at least we hope so! This wedding is really going to be different. For openers we're going to have the ceremony on top of a nearby mountain. Our invitations will read that on any one of three or four days (depending on weather conditions) we will caravan up to the mountaintop and have a sunset wedding.

"We want something unique, that hasn't been manu-factured from a book of church rituals, but a celebration service created for our needs—with words and expressions that will have meaning for us. Every part of our wedding will have a spiritual significance. Before we start up the mountain we want to gather our friends someplace and have communion with a big loaf of bread and then share a cup of wine. During the ceremony we want to wash each other's feet—like Jesus and his disciples. We are going to wear simple clothes—as will our guests. Afterwards we'll have a weiner roast. And later we'll spend the night on the mountain with our closest friends nearby. We think the best place to begin our married life is with a mountaintop perspective."

Rarely have I felt such total absorption in another person's description of an event past, present, or future. It seemed that everyone and everything in the room had disappeared and all that was present were those two beautifully happy faces paying us the supreme compliment of allowing us to hear how Christ was leading them. In a typically open gesture they asked the group assembled to stretch out on the floor seeking Second Sight on anything that might help in their planning. I was thrilled to participate in seeking guidance from the mind of Christ for the wedding of these new age spirits. I knew perfectly well, however, that the parents of the young couple might have some reservations at this departure from tradition, and they did. I was thankful for the Second Sight leading and awareness that was provided throughout this revolutionary experience. We were given to know that God's word to Nancy and Jack was the same as that spoken to Moses: "My presence shall go with thee . . ." (Exod. 33:14, KJV).

After several sessions, a pattern for the wedding celebration was drawn together. What follows is the ceremony used on the occasion of their wedding, that incidentally was attended by both sets of parents and a large gathering of young and old who seemed to enjoy it immensely.

## The Celebration of Marriage

At the time and place agreed upon, the persons who come to be formally joined shall stand hand in hand before the one who will pronounce the blessing of Christ on their marriage. [Obviously the person who officiates must be qualified by the laws of his respective state.]

Facing each other they shall kiss each other's hands. The minister shall speak:

"Let us listen to the silence of God."

After a period of quiet the minister shall say:

"We have come here to celebrate the wedding of two spirits destined by God to be joined together. We praise God for what he is doing in their lives. We thank God for the love that has drawn them together."

The minister shall say first to the man:

"Jack, your love for Nancy is growing with each passing day. Your love shall be like a light in the darkness, and no darkness will ever put it out."

The minister shall say to the woman:

"Nancy, your love for Jack is growing with each passing day. Your love will be like a banquet feast and all who see the joy in your lives will be made happy."

The minister shall say:

"Let us meditate. Let us see Jack and Nancy walking hand in hand. See the light of their love as a great radiance surrounding them, until at last we see only the light—holy and pure as those walking together have gone on ahead. What we now see is the shining afterglow of God's creative love that calls man and woman together and gives a new dimension to life."

The minister shall say:

"The wedding ring is an outward symbol of an inward fact. These two lives are joined in God's love.

"Jack, you may place the ring on Nancy's finger. Nancy you may place the ring on Jack's finger." [They shall continue to hold hands.]

The minister shall say to both parties:

"Please repeat after me: Our love is perfect because God loves us and because we love each other. God's love is eternal."

The minister shall say:

"Christ was a servant. He loved his friends and served them by washing their feet. He who was greatest was willing to do the least."

The minister shall hand Jack a towel, then Nancy a towel. They shall kneel alternately and wash each other's feet. Each shall say to the other prior to the footwashing:

"I serve you with my love."

Then the celebrants shall kneel together facing the minister. He shall say:

"For the love that has drawn Jack and Nancy together we celebrate that they are husband and wife together by the power of God's Holy Spirit."

The minister shall bring forth a cup filled with fresh water and say:

"You may now drink from this wedding cup. The water is like that which bubbles up from eternal life and lives within you."

After each has drunk, the parties shall rise and hold the cup together while the minister reads the 13th chapter of First Corinthians:

"If I speak in the tongues of men and of angels, but have not love, I am a noisy gong or a clanging cymbal. And if I have prophetic powers, and understand all mysteries and all knowledge, and if I have all faith, so as to remove mountains, but have not love, I am nothing. If I give away all I have, and if I deliver my body to be burned, but have not love, I gain nothing.

"Love is patient and kind; love is not jealous or boastful; it is not arrogant or rude. Love does not insist on its own way; it is not irritable or resentful; it does not rejoice at wrong, but rejoices in the right. Love bears all things, believes all things, hopes all things, endures all things.

"Love never ends; as for prophecy, it will pass away; as for tongues, they will cease; as for knowledge, it will pass away. For our knowledge is imperfect and our prophecy is imperfect; but when the perfect comes, the imperfect will pass away. When I was a child, I spoke like a child, I thought like a child, I reasoned like a child; when I became a man, I gave up childish ways. For now we see in a mirror dimly, but then face to face. Now I know in part; then I shall understand fully, even as I have been fully understood. So faith, hope, love abide, these three; but the greatest of these is love."

The benediction shall follow:

"Father, may we be aware that even while on earth we are living spirits who inhabit eternity. We have celebrated the joining of two spirits into a oneness of enterprise. May they be ever open and responsive to your love that has brought them together and your Spirit that gives them life, joy, and peace now and forever. Amen."

The idea of celebrating the wedding bond with a new pattern triggered a desire in me to do the same with other ceremonies through which we celebrate the seasons of life. If there is one thing I have learned in our Second Sight groups, it is that God delights in variety. It is his very nature to be creative. In light of this hopeful perspective I include the following alternatives to what is now available in traditional rituals—perhaps these can be like new wineskins.

## Celebration of Entering Eternal Life

As these words are read let the casket be closed or preferably removed from the room where the people are gathered. The minister shall say:

"Let us pray: Father, we have heard you pronounce through Christ Jesus, I AM the resurrection and the life. We affirm that you are our refuge and strength and that underneath are the everlasting arms. We know that you are our light, our life, and that our ultimate care is with you. Help us in this hour to lift up our eyes to your hills and gain the spiritual perspective to live through these moments in the dark valley. Amen."

The minister shall then read two selections of Scripture from the Old and New Testaments.

"The Lord is my shepherd, I shall not want;
   he makes me lie down in green pastures.
He leads me beside still waters;
   he restores my soul.
He leads me in paths of righteousness
   for his name's sake.
Even though I walk through the valley of the shadow of
      death,
   I fear no evil;

for thou art with me;
    thy rod and thy staff,
    they comfort me.

Thou preparest a table before me
    in the presence of my enemies;
thou anointest my head with oil,
    my cup overflows.
Surely goodness and mercy shall follow me
    all the days of my life;
and I shall dwell in the house of the Lord
    for ever."

(Psalm 23)

" 'You must not let yourselves be distressed—you must hold on to your faith in God and to your faith in me. There are many rooms in my Father's House. If there were not, should I have told you that I am going away to prepare a place for you? It is true that I am going away to prepare a place for you, but it is just as true that I am coming again to welcome you into my own home, so that you may be where I am. You know where I am going and you know the road I am going to take.'

" 'Lord,' Thomas remonstrated, 'we do not know where you're going, and how can we know what road you're going to take?'

" 'I myself am the road,' replied Jesus, 'and the truth and the life. No one approaches the Father except through me. If you had known who I am, you would have known my Father. From now on, you do know him and you have seen him.' "

(John 14:1-3, Phillips)

The minister may offer this meditation:

    There was no home on earth that Jesus loved more than that of Mary, Martha, and Lazarus. I feel sure that whenever he was anywhere near their home in the village of Bethany he would be sure to stop by for a visit.

Once when Jesus was out in the country somewhere preaching, Lazarus became ill. The sisters sent word to Jesus concerning Lazarus's illness in the hope that he would come quickly and heal their brother. But Jesus had to finish the work in which he was involved, so it was a few days before he was able to make his way back to Bethany. In the meantime Lazarus had died, and as Jesus arrived at the little village he found a crowd of mourners weeping and wailing in front of the tomb. Soon enough he learned that this was the grave of his friend Lazarus. Suddenly Mary rushed up to him and said boldly, "Lord, if you had been here, my brother would not have died"—which was, of course, true.

Jesus began to weep. Great tears flowed down his face, so much so that one of the people in the crowd pointed a finger at him saying, "See how much he loved him."

Then Jesus ordered that the stone be moved away from in front of the tomb. He turned his face toward the heavens to pray, and at length shouted into the foul smelly place of death, "Lazarus, come out." And Lazarus came out, ". . . his hands and feet bound with grave clothes and his face muffled with a handkerchief" (John 11:44, Phillips).

My question is this. Why did Jesus weep that day in Bethany? Surely he knew, even while shedding tears, that he would be able to call Lazarus back from death. Why then the expression of grief? I believe he wept because he was calling a man back from a place where there is no more sickness, no more pain, no anxiety, no boredom, no loneliness, no loss or separation—a place where there is no more death. He wept because he was calling a man back from the Father's house—the place of perfection, wholeness, joy, love, reconciliation, peace, and fulfillment. He wept because he was calling a man back from the final destination of everyman's journey—the Homeland!

And that is where your loved one is now—released from the limitations of this existence to be made whole—in the Father's house.

Let us pray:

"Eternal Father, even in this place of sorrow we can see with our mind's eye a great house, out beyond the dimensions of this earth-life. And now we see the lights of that house go on, and a host of friends within are singing and rejoicing. One gone for awhile has returned, and a great reunion is taking place. Father, we release our loved one to you, and await the time when we shall be together again in the Father's house. In the name and nature of Jesus Christ. Amen."

## Graveside Service

If there must be a graveside service, let the following Scripture be read by the minister:

"And I saw the holy city, new Jerusalem, coming down out of heaven, prepared as a bride adorned for her husband; and I heard a great voice out of heaven saying, Behold the tabernacle of God is with men, and he will dwell with them and be their God. And God shall wipe away all tears from their eyes; and there shall be no more death, neither sorrow, nor crying, neither shall there be any more pain: for the former things are passed away."

(Rev. 21:2-4, KJV)

Then the minister shall offer this prayer:

"Almighty God, in whom we live and move and have our being, help us by thy strength to look beyond this place and to see the morning break like a thousand suns. Help us to hear triumphant songs of the resurrection angels singing that the superficial powers of darkness have been put to flight by the death, conquering love, and eternal Spirit of God. Through Christ our Lord. Amen."

## Celebration for Baptism or Dedication of a Child

No celebration of life is more meaningful than that of making vows on behalf of a child that he be given the opportunity of spiritual unfolding through the medium of a responsive home environment.

The parents shall bring their child and stand before the minister at a designated time and place. Witnesses may or may not accompany them and the celebration can be private or before a larger gathering. The minister shall say:

"Each child is born with spiritual music in his life. The music is a unique gift, given for the purpose of bringing a measure of harmony in a disharmonious world. However, the full development and expression of this gift will depend on the ability of the parents to provide the environment in which such music can be expressed. If you who present this child will deal sacramentally with his/her dawning life, a great crescendo of blessing will be given to the world."

The minister shall say to the parents:

"I ask you now in the presence of God: Will you provide a climate of personal love, responsive openness, willing honesty, and the dedicated resolve to go deeper spiritually for the sake of the child you have brought here?"

The parents shall answer:

"I will, Christ being my strength."

The minister shall say:

"As Jesus took a child in his arms and said that of such is the kingdom of God, so I now hold your child and say the same to you."

The minister shall hold the child in such a way that the child can see his parents at all times. The minister shall say:

"(first name of child), in the name of the Father and of the Son and of the Holy Spirit—may you receive the blessing of Christ in and through your life."

The minister may offer this prayer:

"Father, we praise you for the spiritual gift wrapped in the life of this child. May all the music born in his life be expressed, because these who have made certain vows on his behalf are firm in the trust that is theirs by the grace of God through Christ our Lord. Amen."

## Celebration for Blessing a Home

One of the most frequently requested celebration services is for blessing a new home. I can't think of a more important family experience than to gather for a house blessing.

This order of celebration should be performed as soon as a family moves into a house. The officiator, who could be a member of the family, a close friend, or a minister, shall gather the family in the living room and shall read:

"The Lord is in his holy temple, let all the earth keep silence before him. Let us be silent."

After a period of quiet let the officiator continue:

"Father, we gather here to give thanks that this will be our home, and to call on the heavenly hosts to purify and bring all vibrational patterns in this place into a harmonious rhythm. We seek spiritual cleansing of every nook and cranny of this building, that thy perfect will may be done and the light of thy love may give our home the blessing of thy holy presence."

Each member of the family shall go to his appointed room, or the family members shall accompany one another to each room, and together in one chorus of blessing say:

"In the name and through the power of Jesus Christ—let this room be flooded with the cleansing, healing, perfecting light of God's protective love and wholeness. Thank you Father. Amen."

The family shall reassemble in the living room and all join in singing a song of praise such as "O God Our Help in Ages Past," or "Holy, Holy, Holy." They shall then join hands in a circle and pray together the Lord's prayer, followed by such extemporaneous prayers as they may desire.

## Celebration for the Renewal of One's Life

Some Pharisees asked Jesus when the Kingdom of God would come. His answer was: "The Kingdom of God does not come in such a way as to be seen [with outward sight]. No one will say, 'Look, here it is!' or, 'There it is!'; because the Kingdom of God is within you."

(Luke 17:20–21, TEV)

If you have reached the point where you desire with all your heart to experience the Kingdom of God, to deepen your spiritual life and to become what you were purposed to become, the following may be helpful:

Begin where you are. You don't have to go anywhere else. The place where you stand right now is Heaven—no matter how depressing or unpromising it may appear. We must never judge from appearances. There is as much God where you are as in the most perfect spiritual environment on the face of the earth. God is present in all life as the Eternal presence. He is present the moment you recognize him, no matter where that may be. Moses discovered God in the seemingly God-forsaken desert of Midian in the fortieth year of his exile. The I AM of life spoke to him from a burning bush and declared the place where he was standing holy ground.

First, you must recognize and affirm what Jesus taught and what the Christ within expresses, "I came that your joy might be full." In a universal sense the word is "full" —no approximates. This joy enters when a person stops judging himself for wrongdoing of the past or for inadequacy in the present, when he finally stops trying to get himself straightened out through a multitude of justifying devices. Initially you must become aware that all the problems of the past and present cannot be put right by your own endless manipulations. The power to set things in their proper order comes from God, and the channel for this growth in perspective comes through the indwelling Christ.

Second, it is time that you "stir up the gift of God which is within you." Every person has been given a gift of God, and that gift is preeminently Christ. Christ stands at the door of your recognition and knocks, awaiting your response. The Scripture reads, " 'Behold, I stand at the door and knock; if any one [including you] hears my voice and opens the door, I will come in to him and eat with him, and he with me' " (Rev. 3:20).

Third, you must be born again. This is a matter of deliberately lifting your attention from the appearance level of the present tense and concentrating on a "potentiality consciousness." Herein one begins to live on the brink of possibility, knowing that "with God all things are possible." Even in this very moment God can release the forces of a new life if you are willing to receive. This is being born again. It is an awakening from darkness to light, from despair to hope, from belief to knowing, from limited vision to Second Sight. With a born-again perspective, you can see yourself and your situation (no matter how hopeless) as God's opportunity, in that God becomes less your opportunity—to get, grab, and gain— but you become *God's opportunity* to be used for his highest purpose. In fact, you are giving God a new way to reveal himself—through the potentiality of a new creation awaiting expression.

Fourth, you need to be alone for a little while so that you can relax your body, focus your mind, and let these words seep into your consciousness: "Be still and know." In the stillness you will come to know—not the knowing of belief, but the knowing of enlightenment that opens the door to actuality where you receive what is yours to receive. Now rejoice, sing a new song, praise God, dance before him, and celebrate the inward Christ whose love has fulfilled your life.

Perhaps the celebrations suggested in this chapter will inspire others to create new forms for specific situations as disclosed through the focus of Second Sight. If several of my wishes would be granted, one of them would be for church people to sit down and consider whether or not the rituals, creeds, and even hymns used for worship purposes really speak to their need. Perhaps something akin to the important tool used in modern biblical studies called "hermeneutics" (the science of interpretation) could be used for the sake of making our approaches in worship more relevant and inspiring.

# 7

# THE IMPORTANCE
# OF RHYTHM

"Beneath everything there is a basic rhythm of life, and discovering it must be the most important discovery of man's life."

—*An insurance executive, aged 32.*

# THE IMPORTANCE
# OF RHYTHM

A creative young scientist in New York City operates a school for training law enforcement personnel on the use of the polygraph or lie detector. One day, for some reason, his intellectual curiosity was challenged to consider what would happen if he attached his extra-sensitive detecting equipment to something other than a human being. For instance, would the philodendron plant sitting on his desk give off a life force vibrational pattern that could be measured on recording tape?

Deciding to check out his speculations with some concrete experiments, the scientist hooked up the philodendron to his sensitive machinery. Within seconds, much to his delight, he found that the plant was not only sending out a rhythmic impulse pattern but was also reacting to a variety of stimuli —to threat, stress, love, death to another organism in the environment. Even more incredibly, it seemed to respond in emotional interplay with the young scientist himself. In all test situations, the plant made a definite recorded tracing that displayed its sensitivity response to stimuli of different types. I was intrigued to learn that the plant responded as much to the threat of harm as to actual injury inflicted on itself.

The story of this investigation has had a profound influence on my thinking with regard to the effect of varying environmental stimuli on a human being. If, for instance, the relatively simple organism of a philodendron plant is affected by negative influences in its environment, consider what happens when a human being with his extremely complex physical-mental-spiritual structure is exposed to the same influences.

In a meditation group one afternoon, I could not help but note the distinct lack of enthusiasm in one of our members. We had been discussing the philodendron experiment and how negativism can affect a person. Suddenly the downcast one declared quite emotionally, "I feel like I'm under threat. My mother is always giving me this 'hopeless case' look, and even when she's not saying anything or looking at me, I can feel her disapproving thoughts. I'm convinced she doesn't love me. I feel miserable so much of the time—like right now I am coming down with a cold."

We immediately went into meditation, seeking some Second Sight guidance on the problem at hand. One girl visualized a tape like that used on the polygraph machine. She interpreted this to be an in-depth vibrational recording of the downcast young man's life pattern. At first she could see a normal rhythmic tracing, but then the markings became a blur of violent dark impulses. She nearly shouted, "You must get your life back in harmony or you'll be overcome by the darkness." Moving from the appearance to the real, she began speaking of God's plan and purpose for his life.

In my meditation that afternoon, I recalled that the psychologist Dr. Sidney Jourard suggested that the maximum level of health is maintained by the inflow of inspiriting (high moral building) factors while conversely nothing is more detrimental to a person's health than the dispiriting effect of negativism in all of its many aspects. In other words the affect of the rhythmic (flow of positive influences) as set over against the unrhythmic (negative patterns) may be the difference between health and illness.

The face of a minister friend I had visited recently came onto the screen of my mind. He met me at the airport, and we set out on the highway toward his church. Along the way he began pouring out his smoldering anger and deep-seated resentment toward a particular denominational leader whom he bitterly accused of denying him an appointment to a church for which he felt eminently qualified to serve.

"Instead," he stated fiercely, "I was sent to this impossible, unchallenging church out in the middle of nowhere." With fire in his eyes he exploded, "I'll show him. I'll show that dirty, doublecrosser. I'll put this little church on the map. I'll receive more members this year than in the church's entire history. Maybe that will make him take notice of me!"

I have rarely seen a man so choked with rage. All at once his face turned a pasty white, and he almost doubled over the steering wheel. I asked if I could help, but he waved me off. Pulling off to the side of the road he was finally able to tell me of the excruciating pain in his stomach and how he was afraid that he might have an ulcer. Shaking his head sadly he muttered as though to himself, "I can't understand it. Why should I have an ulcer? What have I done to deserve this?" Without a Second Sight perspective of his personal identity in Christ, it had never occurred to him that his negative, unrhythmic hostility was sufficient cause for an ulcer or any other disease.

Another face appeared on the screen of my mind. He

was one of the most enjoyable companions I have known
—a church leader, a prayer group member, and a church
school teacher. He seemed the perfect picture of what a man
with a Christ-centered rhythmic faith should be.

Over a period of time, some negative thoughts began seep-
ing into his consciousness that he rehearsed over and over.
It occurred to him that his wife was more interested in her
church activities (usually prayer groups and church school)
than she was in him. He found it increasingly difficult to
communicate with her about the spiritual life, because she
was racing about, involved in so many activities related to
it, and constantly on the phone talking about it. Then there
was the problem of her attractiveness. It seems that she had
let herself settle somewhat since the early days of their
marriage—some thirty pounds of settling.

At a critical stage of their growing estrangement, along
came a shapely young lady whom he met in a business
situation. She was the antithesis of his wife—young, slim,
attractive, absorbed in his interests and in need of a man.
An affair began that interestingly enough was conducted
quite openly.

I watched my friend take a tremendous emotional beating
that nearly broke my heart. All the need within for a
rhythmic life of right relationships was rebelling against the
present chaos of broken spiritual laws. He became ill and
eventually he was taken to the hospital suffering from what
the doctors later diagnosed as an emotional collapse. While
visiting him one afternoon, I attempted to gain some perspective by asking if he could justify his beliefs with his actions
—if in an ultimate sense this was the life he wished to
present before the face of God.

He cried out in anger, "I'm all right, I'm all right! There

is nothing wrong with what I'm doing. It's my life. I can do what I please."

But none of us can do what we please—not really—not when we have discovered, even in a limited way, the rhythmic order of oneness with Christ.

As we probe the surface levels of life, Second Sight reveals a basic vibrational rhythmic pattern at the heart of all nature. There is at the center of creation a steady rhythmic pulsation like that of a heartbeat or the steady beat of a drum keeping time for dancing or marching feet. Rhythm is the sound of the rolling surf that comes and goes with steady cadence, or the majestic tick-tock, tick-tock, of a grandfather clock. It is the sight of darkness and light never failing to keep their own period of a day. It is the seasons following in perfect order and predictable sequence. Rhythm is seen in the fluid movement of an athlete who, through disciplined effort, has mastered the diverse skills of his sport and is able to blend the separate entities into an overall demonstration of what appears to be an effortless rhythmic flow. Perhaps the one thing that distinguishes the best athletes from the merely good performers is that the great ones possess a rhythm so constant it appears as poetry in motion.

Second Sight sensitivity to the pulsebeat of creativity gives one the free flow feeling of having discovered the elemental groove of rightness. Love does feel good; so does peace, joy, creative work, study, play—and of course spiritual development, because this is the nature of our being. Herein is rhythm.

Late one night I meditated on the "elemental groove" feeling I had experienced earlier that evening during the concert performance of a famous pianist. The musician hit a stride of expression that built to a magnetic swell, catching up the audience in a oneness of exalted feeling, a rhythmic togetherness. What the performer had done on our behalf through his performance was to reveal the presence of a magnificent composer. But this was no easy, automatic accomplishment; it came as the result of long disciplined hours not only devoted to interpreting the composer's structural composition but seeking to get in touch with his very spirit.

As I responded to the masterful performer's art, in essence I was participating in the spirit of the music that had been so magnificently channeled through the artist. Because of the pianist's inspired playing, I was able to see through notes, measures, bars, instrument, orchestra, stage, lights, concert hall—to the inner structure of the music expressed with such unusual artistry. In the magic of those moments, the performer had become more than just a part of this musical production. His long sensitive fingers sweeping over the keyboard, the depth of his concentration, the dramatic move of head and body, all accelerated an unreal sense of identity between musician and music. In this mystic involvement, it seemed the man on stage had constructed a musical bridge over which I was invited to join him in the purest sort of rhythmic oneness. It was an extraordinary moment in the heights.

The same phenomenon takes place in the sports world. The term *momentum* is often used to describe an athletic team that catches fire and begins to perform in flawless fashion, becoming practically invincible. This is another demonstration of mounting the flow of an irresistible rhythmic current that leads one beyond the sphere of limitation into a wholeness of expression. But this requires much discipline in penetrating the surface level of unrhythmic appearance.

Lately I have been investigating the effect of various colors on a person's total organism. In our Second Sight groups I have continually raised questions concerning one's personal response to specific colors, and have been amazed at the similarity of the answers, at least in general categories of reference. Second Sighters seeking an environmental color harmony that would lead toward a more rhythmic flow of life are increasingly beginning to select their surrounding colors at home, work, play, etc. in accordance with the results of our research.

Obviously there is a tremendous need for more sophisticated inquiry into the effect of color in a multiplicity of areas. Genuine value would be derived from color research that is not subject to artistic caprice or other subjective influences but is grounded in a long-term scientific study under the strictest clinical conditions. Perhaps when sufficient evidence is collected, even the old age public may be convinced of the beneficial results that can be derived when color is put to work in the service of mankind. But until the perfect comes, the imperfect will have to do. With that in mind the following color list has been prepared with full recognition that it by no means exhausts the subject and merely represents a working guide that should be evaluated from time to time as Second Sight dictates.

*Red.* Red is the action color that excites and stimulates a person to dynamic activity. But stimulation can be overdone if the red is too brilliant. This color is often a positive recuperative factor when viewed at length by a hospital patient lacking the will to recover. In such situations I urge that red flowers, books with red jackets, red vases—anything red but not overwhelmingly large be put in plain sight of the patient.

*Orange.* More compatible than red, orange and its companion, peach, tend to work out extremely well as a home color, particularly in places where food is prepared and eaten. Peach also does well in a hospital room or business office. Slightly toned-down orange is extremely compatible in most places where there is an abundance of physical activity.

*Yellow.* Yellow is widely used in traffic control mainly because it gains quick attention. Brilliant yellow like bright red can be overused and may tend toward a nervous response. On the other hand pastel yellow is a happy, inspiring color with no adverse effect.

*Green.* Green is the ideal background color for creative relaxation, study, discussion, and spiritual development activities. It is a restful refreshing hue, producing a soothing, quieting influence. Green is the ideal color for a bedroom, den, or living room. With a touch of blue and gray, it has been a fortunate color for our own home environment.

*Blue.* Light blue is emotionally a low-key color that does not give the best results where physical activities occur. In some ways blue can depress the energy-producing aspect of a person and lead to a sort of detachment. This could be helpful in some meditative activity. Dark blue should be used sparingly because it tends toward melancholy.

*Purple or Violet.* Purple is the shade of ascendancy. It is best used in a meditation room, chapel, or sanctuary in brief exposures. If used with discretion, purple in a sick room can point people toward the highest aspirations of wholeness.

*White.* White is the classic ceiling color for all rooms due to its heightened projection toward perfection.

*Black.* In small doses the non-color black can present a restful contrast to an excess of color in an environment, but it must be used cautiously.

*Brown.* An underfoot color, brown does well in cold, austere industrial situations as a reminder of man's need to maintain contact with the good earth.

*Gray.* Gray can be used as a blend to neutralize most colors and make them more accommodating to the aesthetic needs of a given situation.

The balanced use of color is far more important to maintaining an effective life experience than most of us realize. I believe there is a prevalent day-to-day need for specific color absorption as we move through our weekly schedules—that is, if we are to function in a rhythmic fashion. Taking into consideration the normal cycle of a person's body, mind, and spirit needs, a friend suggested that on each weekday a person wear the following colors to some extent, whether it be a tie, stockings, shirt, scarf, belt, etc. He suggested the following:

| Monday | Red |
|---|---|
| Tuesday | Orange |
| Wednesday | Yellow |
| Thursday | Green |
| Friday | Blue |
| Saturday | Purple |
| Sunday | White |

Whatever the therapeutic effect of color, if it helps to provide an environment conducive to the development of Second Sight, it is well worth the experimentation.

A father I knew claimed to love his two sons equally. Yet

he invariably referred to one as "his bright kid" and the other as "the dummy." In all IQ tests taken through elementary and high school the sons ranked about equal, but in their actual classroom performance the son who was frequently reminded of his brightness received significantly higher letter grades than the brother who was chided as a dummy.

Love might best be defined as seeking the highest good of another. If a positive force field of expectation is sent out on behalf of another, this often has the effect of motivating that person to find his natural rhythm and perform on a higher (than normal) level of efficiency. No doubt you have had the experience of being with certain people whose expectancy level for you was so high that during the time spent with them you were filled with new ideas, stimulating conversation, and a warm feeling of heightened self-esteem. You were literally lifted into a rhythmic groove by your friends loving you toward becoming what you could and should be. I am convinced that a rhythmic life is the outgrowth of expectantly creative, redemptive love . . . person to person . . . that has flowed in from the universal expectant, creative, redemptive love of God.

Once in a meditative experience I was transported backward in time to an almost forgotten episode. I began reliving the night my father gave permission for me to borrow his new car so that I could attend a high school football banquet at a state lodge five miles from our town. With six enthusiastic passengers urging me on, I decided to check out the vehicle's maximum speed. Rounding a bend in the narrow road I was startled to see that we were bearing down on a hay wagon blocking the flow of traffic from both directions. Even in the late twilight hour I caught a glimpse of a farmer nonchalantly swinging his pitchfork, tossing hay in a barn that appeared incredibly close to the road. Unable to bring the car to an immediate halt I cut the steering wheel sharply to avoid a direct collision. We careened down through a wide-mouthed ditch narrowly missing a culvert, became airborne, and at last hit the ground bouncing uncontrollably from side to side, crashing through fences, plowing over small trees, and coming to rest in the middle of a cornfield. Miraculously, the battered, broken car was standing upright, although on four deflated tires, covered with mud and scratches. Fortunately no one was injured.

With indescribable reluctance I walked through the gathering dusk to a nearby farm house and phoned my father. My mother took the message and closed the conversation with ominous brevity: "Your father will be there shortly." I rejoined the others at the scene of the accident, and after examining the wrecked car one more time, I stood in deadly silence like a condemned prisoner waiting for the executioner to appear.

In a relatively short period, lights began to sweep across the horizon. Far off I could hear the mournful wail of police sirens coming in our direction. A line of whirling red lights appeared close at hand. One by one the cars began to arrive from the sheriff's office, the state police, the newspaper, a local radio patrol, and a dispatched garage wrecker. Brakes screeched, doors slammed, and people began moving toward us from different directions, guided by the streaming rays of flashlights. Soon the beams of light were rudely stripping away the veil of darkness, converging at length on my father's damaged automobile that now stood naked for all to see.

This was unquestionably the worst moment of my life. I felt nauseous. I hated myself. I wanted to die. It was far worse than being tackled for a loss in the championship game, or hearing some silly girls giggle at my round bowl haircut inflicted by an inexperienced barber, or explaining inadequately to my mother why I had flunked high school algebra.

The first person I saw walking directly toward the disaster area was my father. The dreaded moment had arrived sooner than I had expected. I felt cold and numb and wished that he could have found me lying wounded in a pool of blood— anything to compensate him for his loss . . . to restore the balance I feared lost in our relationship . . . to recover the rhythm.

In my reverie I saw again his face as I had seen it that night in the reflection of crisscross lights. He wore an expression I had never seen before or since. With complete justification he could have screamed at me in a rage of anger, cursed and denounced me with impunity. I would have understood and accepted, whatever the condemnation. Instead there were tears in his eyes. He reached out and wrapped his arms about me. We stood like that for several moments. No words were spoken that I recall. There was just the knowing that because he still loved me the rhythm had been restored. His Second Sight perspective of overcoming love brought healing and wholeness; and I shall always be grateful.

Nothing breaks down this love rhythm faster than making value judgments on other people without a love translation through Second Sight. When we evaluate people solely on the basis of color, nationality, religion, age, vocabulary, school, job, car, house, and clothes, a rigid caste system of group identity is established that separates people—me or us against them. This unloving, unrhythmic attitude that tolerates no diversity has spawned more evil in the world than any other I know. There can be no communication between individuals or groups if they are forever saying to themselves, "We will not be open to someone who is different from us."

One of the beautiful things about the Second Sight groups is that there is no sense of stereotyped individual distinctions when we are moving toward an experience of the spirit, though we are from diverse backgrounds. We are simply one in a rhythmic awareness. We share a love relationship in the Spirit that brings a harmonious benefit for the good of all. When consciousness is lifted, what appears to separate people becomes unimportant.

I am convinced that few people can measure up to their God-given potential unless an air of expectancy is generated by those around them. Those who care enough to look with Second Sight beneath a person's appearance level to see a potential spiritual identity and are willing to build on this can perform a ministry of love that calls forth the highest response in another. No human effort is more significant, because this is a ministry that we share directly with God.

One of the most appealing biblical characters is the New Testament personality Barnabas. His life reveals a blessed harmony because it was filled with self-giving, creative, reconciling love. When the Apostle Paul undertook his first missionary journey, Barnabas accompanied him, as did a young man named John Mark. Apparently John Mark did not work out very well, because he deserted the team early in their travels and took a boat back home, much to Paul's chagrin. In fact Paul was so profoundly disappointed in Mark that when it was time to plan his second missionary effort he let it be known that he had no intention of giving the young man a second chance. Barnabas attempted to

intercede, but to no avail. Paul was adamant in his objection
to John Mark's accompanying them. Barnabas, however,
employing his Second Sight magnificently, recognized something in the young man that Paul had missed. In fact, he
went so far as to break with his old friend and team up with
the former deserter so that they could set out on a missionary
venture of their own.

Unquestionably this was a pivotal point in the young
man's life—a loving hand reached out to touch his sagging
shoulder and restore his life to its creative rhythm. Eventually
the day came when Barnabas's trust was thoroughly vindi-
cated, for it was that same John Mark who wrote one of the
best-known books in human history—The Gospel according
to Mark. Saint Mark he is called. The Second Sight love of
Barnabas released a flow of rhythmic vibrations in the young
Gospel writer's life that provided a blessing beyond words
and released a gift beyond measure.

A Unitarian friend once observed, "Don't you think it
was rather pompous of Jesus to go around saying, 'I am The
Way, The Truth and The Life'?" Following a Second Sight
meditation I told him that, far from exercising his ego, it
seemed to me Jesus was revealing the secret of his remarkably
rhythmic life—a life flowing with consistency of purpose
and emptying itself in a spiritual ministry that has led countless persons into a new dimension of discovering who they
really are.

I am convinced that the Christ Spirit is the creative presence within each of us supporting and renewing our lives
against the background of God's creative plan and purpose.
When Jesus said, "I am the life," he was not speaking of his
external physical self. Rather he was being spoken through
by the same Spirit that spoke to Moses when he stood by a

burning bush in the desert of Midian. Moses asked the speaker to identify himself, and the voice answered "I AM who I AM" (Exod. 3:14). That "I AM" expression is heard in other Old Testament references but it reaches the zenith of its expression when we hear Jesus say, "I am the vine," "I am the bread," "I am the door," "I am the resurrection," "I am the good shepherd," "before Abraham was, I am.' "[1]

Before Jesus was removed from the earth scene, he said to his followers with his Godlike perspective, "It is to your advantage that I go away, for if I do not go away, the Counselor will not come to you" (John 16:7). The coming of the Counselor, or the Holy Spirit, marks the beginning of a spiritual invasion destined to take up life not in just a few chosen ones but to enter the life stream of each man, to be all in all and for all who will receive what is theirs to receive. Within each of us is a capacity for response to the Spirit, because at the taproot of every man there abides a scaled-down counterpart spirit of the Creator who made man in his own image. Obviously a man can choose to ignore this aspect of his inner being, but the potentiality is still present, as is one's latent Second Sight.

We should not be put off by such biblical expressions as "Christ in you . . . ," "the kingdom of God is within you," and "God created man in his own image." Or by Tennyson's explaining that "Closer is He than breathing, and nearer than hands and feet." Such expressions simply reveal a spiritual identity derived from the same Spirit that spoke his I AM to Moses, pronounced it again in the life of Jesus, and is available through the Holy Spirit to each of us. Awareness of our true identity can become like an inflow of harmonious

1. John 15:1,5; 6:35; 10:7; 11:25; 10:11; 8:58; see also 14:6.

realization that will give a universal reference to all our living.

Now and then, in a Second Sight breakthrough, I have experienced the delightful sense of peace and relatedness with the natural world that manifests itself in a feeling of a deep kinship with all creation. More particularly, I feel related to the same I AM Spirit who called the world into being, who addressed the prophets and holy men of antiquity, who spoke through Jesus of Nazareth, and who speaks through the Christ (I AM) within, calling me by my first name and affirming my life.

In this regard I know who I AM. I feel no urgency to say my creed with impeccable correctness, to read my Bible for the sole purpose of gaining a concrete almost physical relationship with the historical Jesus. I have no compulsion to crawl through a scriptural time tunnel in order to discover my Lord, or to spend more time attempting to relive his landmark death rather than celebrating his eternal life. I simply cannot be involved in the old age mental gymnastics which desperately attempt to make Christ real through a galaxy of external means, when I know he is alive and real in the eternal *now*. And those who have found a dimension of his being within have discovered a magnificent contemporary purposefulness extending from the present scene forward into the immensities of God's infinite perfection and glory.

Jesus once said to a Samaritan woman, "Whoever drinks the water I will give him will never be thirsty again. For my gift will become a spring *in the man himself*, welling up into eternal life" (John 4:14, Phillips). Experiencing the meaning and rhythm of these words cannot be superficially contrived or manufactured, no matter how dedicated our theological intent.

The phone rang one morning. It was a distraught woman uptight, terribly disturbed. She began the conversation hesitantly, "Ah . . . Mr. Gilmore . . . ah . . . Pastor Gilmore . . . ah . . . Dr. Gilmore . . . ah . . . I don't know what to call you . . ."

"Try Don," I said.

She paused, as though gathering her thoughts. "I am a Christian, but my faith isn't helping me any; I'm just eaten up with worry. I'm afraid my husband is being lured away from me by a woman in your church. I've never been so upset. I feel I'm on the verge of a collapse."

After a bit of questioning, I succeeded in getting her to name the woman involved. While it was true that she was a member of our church, I was just as convinced that this woman was not now nor ever had been the least bit romantically involved with her husband. I attempted to reassure her of this fact, but she still kept repeating, "I'm so upset, so worried. Can you help me get over this worry?"

I paused, seeking a Second Sight reflection on whatever might be of help. "Lord help me penetrate the darkness of this problem," I prayed inwardly, "and help me catch sight of a redemptive solution."

Finally a stream of consciousness came into view and I said to the woman, "First, I want you to put on your old clothes and run around the block."

I could hear her nervously clearing her throat on the other end of the line. "Run, did you say run?" She sounded perplexed. "I'm sorry but I can't run anymore. I haven't run since I was a little girl in grade school."

"That's all right," I reassured. "You can run a little bit. If you can't run at least walk fast, but by all means walk until you are tired."

There was no answer.

"Second," I said this strongly for emphasis, "I want you to take a long soaking shower and while you are doing so, think to yourself, *This running water is washing away my worry and cleansing me from all anxiety.*

"Third, dry off, put on your clothes, get in the car, and drive way out in the country. Along the way, search for the largest, most formidable looking tree you can find. Once you have found it, get out of the car, stand in front of the tree, and contemplate it."

"Pardon me," she asked in a puzzled voice, "but did you say contemplate?"

"Yes," I replied. "You must assume that the tree has a message for you. Please notice that it is doing precisely what God wants it to with singleness of purpose by sending its roots trustfully down into the good earth for nourishment with the assurance that it will be cared for. A tree does not question God's steadfast love and attention. It does not worry. It simply lives in the peace of being where it belongs and doing what it was called to do. Let the tree speak to you. That's contemplation."

"Oh," she responded faintly.

"Fourth, is there someone else besides the woman you mentioned with whom you have had a falling out?"

"Yes," she answered.

"Then I want you to go to this person and tell them that you want to be reconciled, even if it means that you apologize first.

"Fifth, I want you to do something creative. Have you ever done any writing?"

"Well," she said, "not since high school."

"Do you realize how many markets there are for articles of

all descriptions on all kinds of subjects?" I suggested she get a writers' guide on where to market her material.

"But I don't much like to write," she protested.

"Well then, get some art supplies and do some painting."

"No, I'm no good at drawing things. But a long time ago I built a bird feeder. It wasn't much, but I was so proud of it."

"Beautiful!" I exclaimed. "Build another one. Build six of them. At last when you crawl into bed after this long exhausting day, I want you to say these words, 'The Lord is in his holy temple, let all the earth keep silence before him.' " She was very quiet. "Do you know what those words mean?" I asked.

"Well," she replied "I've heard them said in church. Does it have to do with God being in the church? Usually the choir sings those words at the beginning of the service."

"Doesn't it mean something more than that?" I asked. "What is the temple of God?"

She was quiet for awhile, then answered thoughtfully, "I once remember reading in the Bible that our bodies are temples of God."

"That's it," I almost shouted. "Go on."

"And if the Lord is in his holy temple . . . could that mean that the Lord is in me? But that's so hard to believe."

"That's where he is," I told her. "The kingdom of God is in you. He is beyond you in a universal sense, but he is in you too—like the lark in the air and the air in the lark. And you are carrying around inside your being the answer to every problem you will ever meet—even now the prescription for your anxiety. The almighty, all-powerful, all-loving Lord is in his (not yours but his) holy temple. Let all (your worries, anxieties, cares) the earth (your earth, your common life) keep silence before him."

"Thank you" she said, "Thank you! I feel so much better."
The phone clicked as she hung up.

What she had meant by saying, "I feel so much better,"
was simply that the rhythm had been restored as her life
forces began functioning in a balance—body, mind, and
spirit.

Perhaps you might try the pattern just outlined in seeking
the universal background of God's plan and purpose for your
life. It is an inescapable fact that when we arrive at the
Second Sight perspective, life is viewed with unclouded
eyes to see its possibilities, its opportunities, and above all the
source of its mastery. The rhythmic ones have discovered a
life flow within, and their outward environment has become
a mirror, faithfully reflecting what is happening internally.
So it will be for discerning ones of the New Age now coming
in. Perhaps they will become our teachers and help us realize
anew that God is never without a witness to any age, least of
all this one.